P9-AFB-284

CREATIVE PAPER CRAFTS

in color

CHESTER JAY ALKEMA

STERLING PUBLISHING CO., INC. NEW YORK

STERLING CRAFTS BOOKS

Block & Silk Screen Printing
Cardboard Crafting
Carpentry for Children
Ceramics—and How to Decorate Them
Craft of Woodcuts
Creating from Scrap
Creative Claywork
Creative Embroidery
Creative Enamelling & Jewelry-Making
Creative Leathercraft
Creative Paper Crafts in Color
Designs—And How to Use Them
How to Make Things Out of Paper
Knitting Without Needles
Make Your Own Mobiles
Making Mosaics
Original Creations with Papier Mâché
Papier Mâché—and How to Use It
Plastic Foam for Arts and Crafts
Printing as a Hobby
Prints—from Linoblocks and Woodcuts
Quilting as a Hobby
Sculpture for Beginners
Stained Glass Crafting
Tin-Can Crafting
Types of Typefaces
Weaving as a Hobby

Sterling Publishing Co., Inc.
419 Park Avenue South, New York 10016
British edition published in Great Britain and the Commonwealth by
The Oak Tree Press, Ltd., 116 Baker St., London, W.1.
Manufactured in the United States of America

Library of Congress Catalog Card No.: 67-27751

CONTENTS

Foreword

There are few art materials more economical, more available, more delightful or more satisfying to the craftsman—young or old—than paper.

The purpose of this book is to offer inspiring ideas. These will provide the background for everyone interested in exploring the numerous fascinating, creative uses of paper in two- and three-dimensional forms.

Some of the projects in this book are very simple to execute and are suitable for children in the primary grades. Others require a more difficult process of construction and are best suited for older children and adults. The important point is that the projects are designed to challenge the creative talents of everyone—regardless of age, level of development or previous experience.

The reader does not have to copy—and should not copy—exactly. To be creative in an art activity, a true artist must make a statement which is highly personal. The many and varied projects offered here are designed to stimulate explorations that are unique and discoveries that are personal. The art products of an individual or group will differ in size, method of construction, color and subject matter.

The book may well serve as a guide for classroom teachers who frequently find themselves limited by supplies and tools, or the person who is involved in recreational programs of a diverse nature. However, the hobbyist, the craftsman who enjoys making things, and anyone who wishes to find a creative means of expression, will welcome this book.

Chester Jay Alkema

Illus. 1. A paper mosaic butterfly. (See Chapter 4.)

PART I: PAPER IN TWO DIMENSIONS

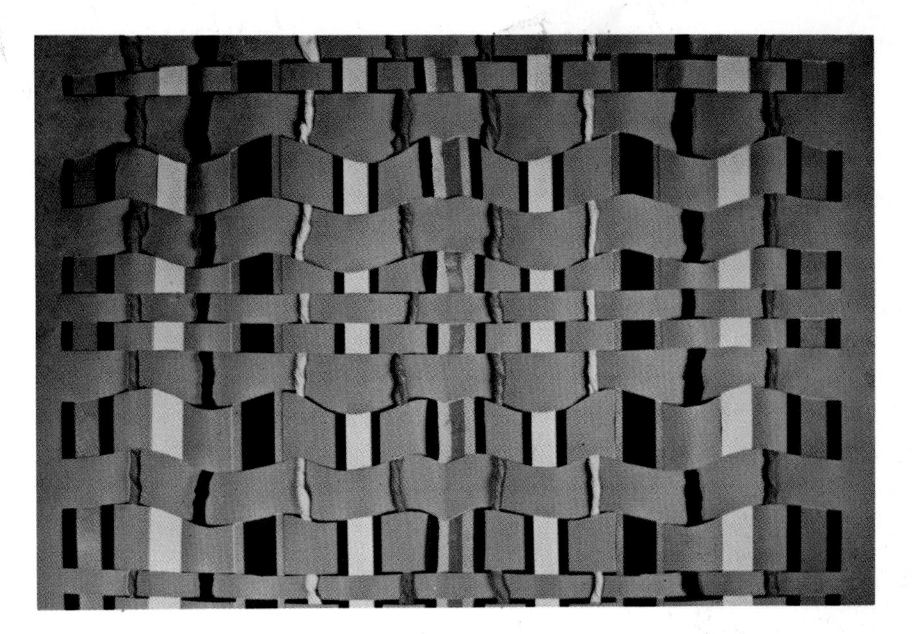

Illus. 2. Paper and other material of various colors and textures are woven together to make this pleasing design.

1. Weaving with Paper

Weaving of paper strips is a fascinating occupation and a delightful craft for children and adults. While the weaving of wool and cloth dates back thousands of years, you will find the craft of paper weaving a simple and effective means of creating both decorative and functional objects.

Woven paper articles are two-dimensional. When weaving, you make and organize your flat surface in one operation. In the pictures, you will notice that design, texture and pattern capture the viewer's interest from the standpoint of touch and sight—the appeal is to both the *visual* and *tactile* senses of the beholder. The objects woven have pleasing color relationships and distribute light and dark areas in an interesting and balanced way.

In Illus. 2, orange and yellow crepe paper, twisted into narrow cords, black rug yarn and paper strips are woven into a green-colored paper loom. In some areas, you will note that overlapped strips were woven in one, single operation. A narrow band of black velvet has been placed over a wider strip of orange paper. This overlapping color scheme is balanced on both sides of the design. On the extreme left and right sides, the opposite color scheme was applied to the overlapping strips: a narrow orange paper strip was placed over a wider black strip of velvet ribbon. The exact middle vertical strip reveals a narrow strip of orange tissue placed over a wider strip of yellow construction paper, and both are pasted against a third, larger, black, velvet ribbon.

Illus. 3. Cutting strips in a folded piece of construction paper to make the warp of a loom.

MAKING A FOLDED PAPER LOOM

In weaving, the loom is threaded with warp, strands that run in a vertical direction. The warp is interlaced with weft, strands that run horizontally.

Fold a 9 x 12 inch sheet of construction paper in the exact middle. Holding your scissors perpendicular to this fold, cut slits, which should terminate about one inch or "two fingers away" from the edges opposite the paper's fold (Illus. 3). These slits provide the warp for the loom. Unfold the loom as shown in Illus. 4, and you are now ready to weave horizontal strips (held in the right hand) in and out of the vertical slits. Illus. 5 shows an almost completed project. Here, a checkerboard pattern has been avoided in several ways: by varying the space between each slit, by not weaving strips through each slit, and by weaving over more than one slit. Notice the resulting shapes—some small,

Illus. 4. The unfolded paper is now a loom, ready for weaving.

Illus. 5. Using dark blue and white horizontal strips, the woven mat is nearly complete.

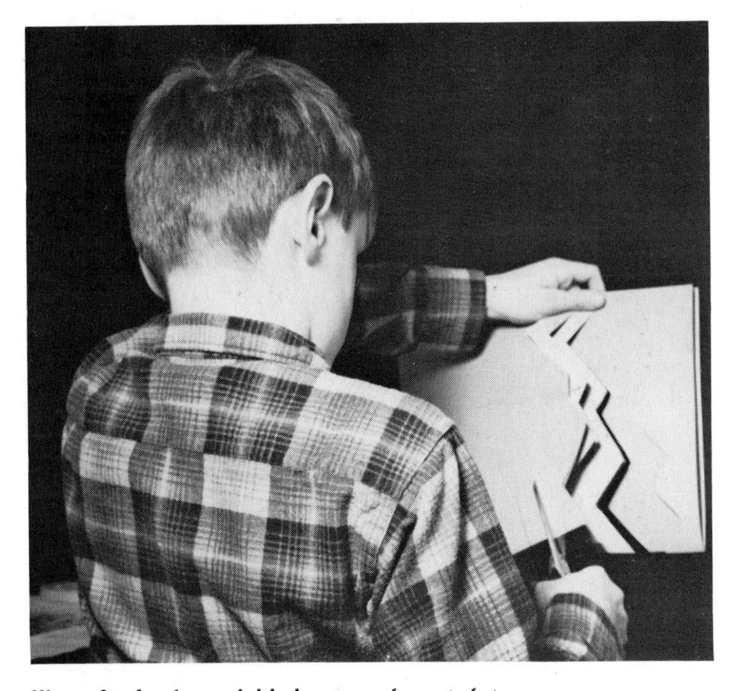

Illus. 6. Again a folded paper is cut into strips, this time making the warp into a zigzag design.

some large. The colors—white, light blue and dark blue—combine to add still more variety.

Illus. 6 shows a different approach. You can cut *zigzag* lines into your folded paper loom. As before, the slits should end about an inch from the fold. Illus. 7 shows the finished product. Try to vary the width of the paper strips and avoid a steady in-and-out weaving.

A design is almost always symmetrical when slits are cut into a folded sheet of paper. Varying widths of the inserted paper strips may distract somewhat from a perfect right- and left-hand balance, but even so, the design will display similarities on either side of the loom's central fold. On the next page, Illus. 8 and Illus. 10 further illustrate how variety and exciting patterns and shapes can be achieved even though they may be symmetrical. These two projects are the result of cutting *diagonal* slits into a folded paper loom.

Illus 7. The zigzag warp can result in this kind of pattern.

Illus. 8. A warp made with diagonal and straight lines can give this effect.

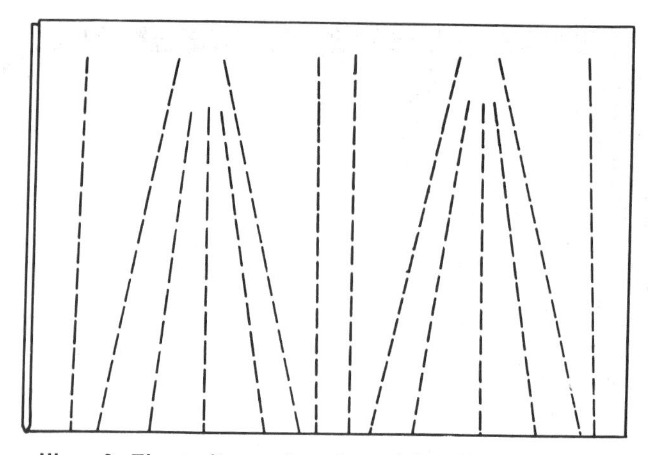

Illus. 9. These diagonal and straight slits were cut to form the warp in Illus. 8.

Illus. 10. Diagonal and curved slits cut into a folded red loom combine to give a radiating design when yellow and blue strips are woven across.

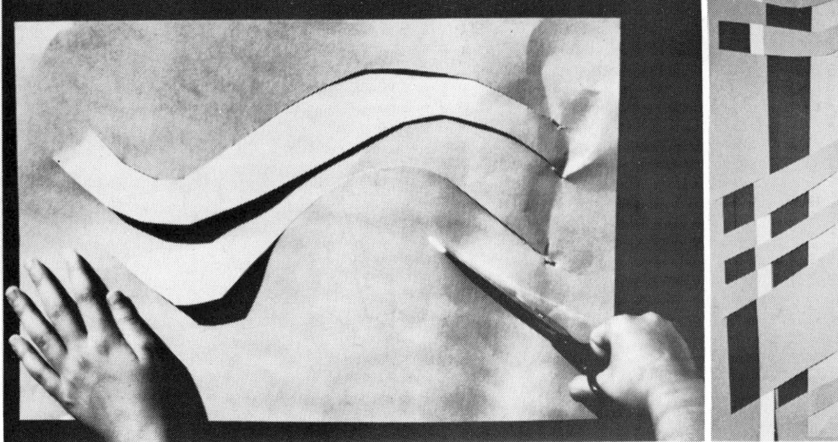

Illus. 11.

Illus. 12.

A NON-FOLDED PAPER LOOM

You are now ready to make designs on a *non-folded* paper loom, which will produce asymmetrical patterns. As shown in Illus. 11, you can cut wavy slits in your large piece of paper. The result (Illus. 12) is a rhythmic flow of lines. In this project, black and white strips are woven into a grey-colored loom.

Illus. 13. Wide yellow and white strips, threaded across a black, non-folded loom with widely spaced slits, make a design which has exciting colors and shapes. Notice the black and white border surrounding the pattern.

Illus. 13 shows a striking example of asymmetrical balance achieved on a non-folded loom.

One of the effects an artist strives for is variety in shape and size. Compare Illus. 14 and Illus. 15. At first glance, Illus. 14 appears to be composed of large shapes, but notice how many little shapes are formed by the bigger ones. Curves, straight lines, long rectangles, squares, shapeless shapes all make up this attractive design. The use of color does much here to enhance and emphasize pattern. While Illus. 15 has many repetitious shapes, their slight variance, placement and brightly contrasting colors make this an effective and pleasing design. It is often through repetition that an artist is able to balance his composition. Repetition and balance are two principles of good design, as you can clearly see in Illus. 16.

Illus. 14. Cutting the warp of a non-folded paper loom produced this asymmetrical design. The two middle white strips cutting across the light blue give the effect of streams of light.

Illus. 15. Narrow dark blue and coral strips in a light blue loom create a tighter pattern, and zigzags, curves and shapes of different sizes provide variety and interest.

Illus. 16. Rounded "bumps" connected by straight lines were used to cut the warp of this black loom. The longer you look at it, the more shapes you will discover.

Illus. 17. This is how the slits were cut to form the warp of the loom shown in Illus. 16.

Illus. 18. Notice how well balanced these shapes and colors are. Compare with Illus. 16. The effect here is the result of evenly spacing diagonal lines when cutting the warp of the yellow loom, and alternating red and black strips of equal width across the loom.

Illus. 19. Across a lavender paper loom a combination of blue and white lace ribbon, white paper, unravelled binder twine, and string has been woven to give this unusual design.

WEAVING WITH DIFFERENT MATERIALS

Up until now you have been weaving with just construction paper. Paper weaving is even more rewarding when various kinds of paper are used. You can produce rectangular-shaped woven articles that will serve functional purposes—placemats, table runners or mats beneath a lamp in the middle of a table.

Heavy, light, rough, smooth, transparent, opaque, dull and intense papers all help to enrich the tactile and visual experiences. Besides construction paper, you can use poster paper, crepe paper, metallic, cellophane or tissue paper, Japanese rice paper and tagboard—separately or in combination.

Materials other than paper might be woven into slits on the paper loom. Illus. 2 at the beginning of the chapter is an example of how you can use many ordinary materials to enhance a paper weaving project. You might make use of some odd bits of white rick-rack trim as in Illus. 20. The zigzag shapes provided by the rick-rack add a pleasing contrast to the straight, vertical lines made by the slits and paper strips. To attain an effect similar to that of Illus. 20, cut straight and diagonal slits into a folded paper loom. Use colors that will add to the visual impact of such an unusual design.

In Illus. 21 black, yellow and orange strips of rick-rack; red, brown, maroon and yellow pipe cleaners; and yellow and olive paper strips of various widths are woven into a neutral green paper loom. Notice how you can vary the rick-rack by using small and large strips, and the pipe cleaners by interrupting one color with another—where a brown cleaner disappears, it reappears yellow.

Remember, there are many everyday, weavable materials you can employ—shoelaces, bias binding, hair ribbons, even grass!

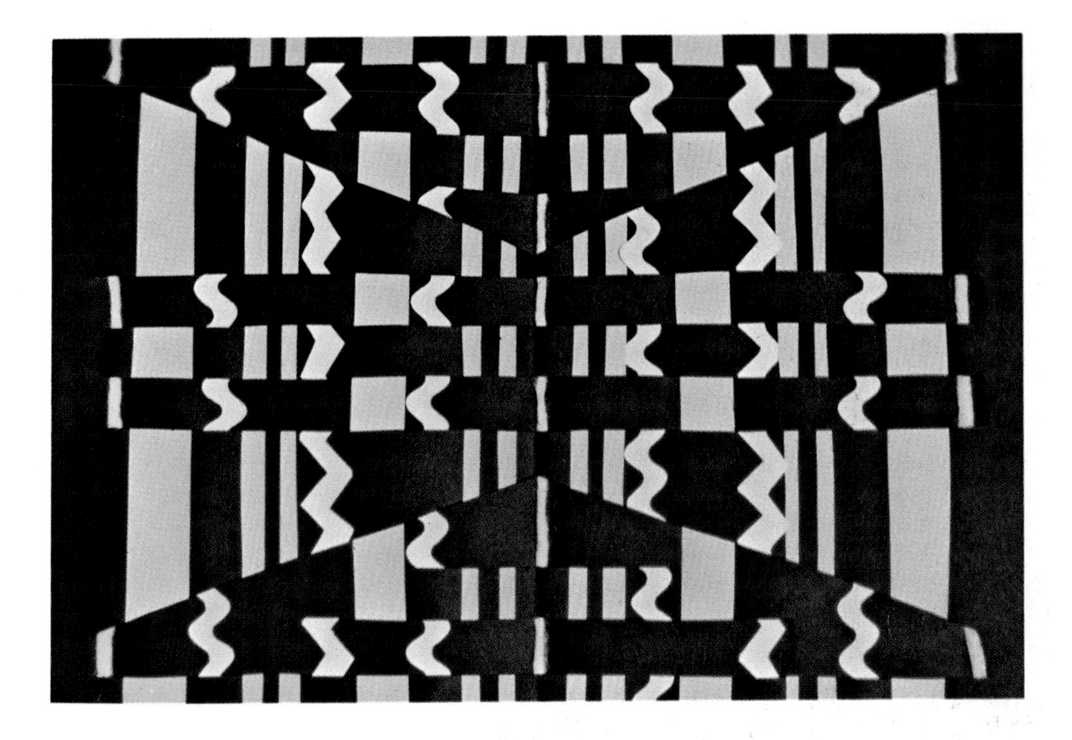

Illus. 20. A green paper loom containing white and yellow paper strips, and white rick-rack. Notice the many ways the pattern proves symmetrical.

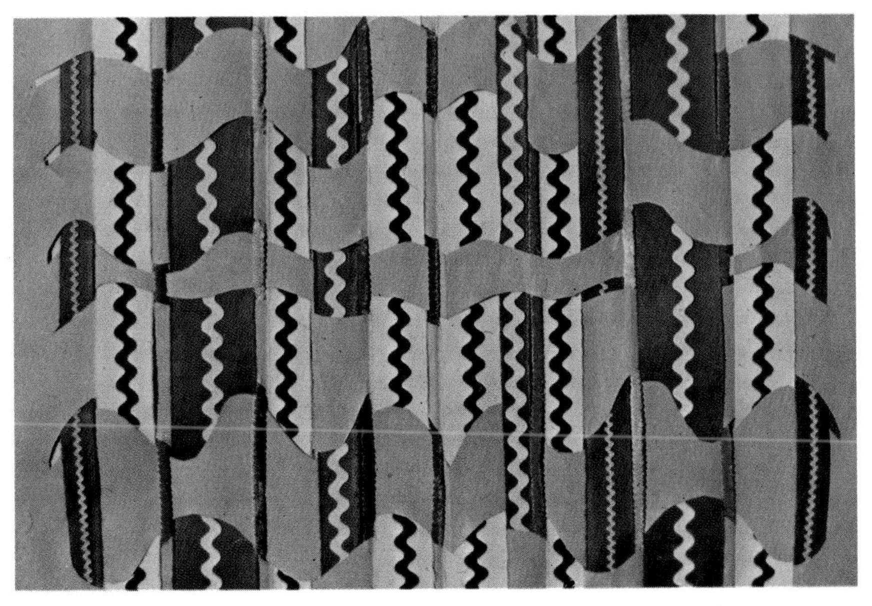

Illus. 21. Rick-rack, pipe cleaners and paper strips are combined to give an Indian blanket effect.

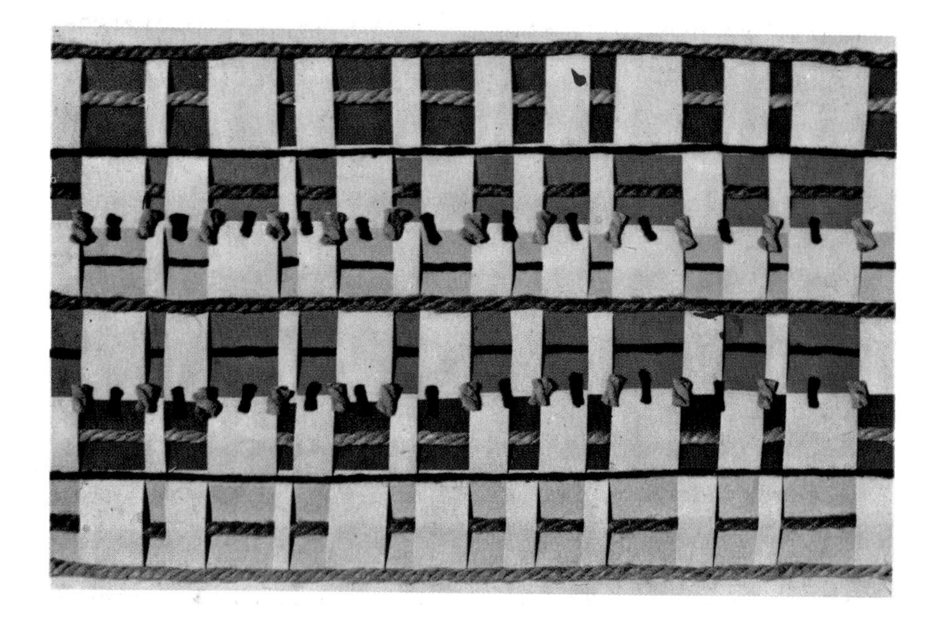

Illus. 22. Brown and blue yarn and rug yarn superimposed on blue, orange and brown strips of paper lie beneath a grey paper lattice. Small bits of black and blue rug yarn are glued on to the surface of the design to add variety.

THREE-DIMENSIONAL DESIGNS

Two-dimensional paper designs need not stay flat—you might sculpture one into a three-dimensional cylinder to create a decorative *stabile*, a kind of stationary mobile or decoration.

You could start out by cutting diagonal slits into a folded sheet (Illus. 25) of paper. Our stabile design is made on a black loom. Weave your strips in the same way as before (Illus. 26). The finished pattern, with twisted crepe paper cords added to the brown and yellow strips of paper, is shown in Illus. 24.

Next, form the flat design into a cylindrical shape. Secure the opposite edges of the paper loom together with brass paper fasteners. The completed stabile is shown in Illus. 27.

Illus. 23. In this blue paper loom are a variety of unusual materials. Look closely and you will find a black and coral necktie, a white zipper, strips of tinfoil and a strip of red mesh from a vegetable bag!

Illus. 24. The V-shaped, flat design is ready to be formed into a cylinder.

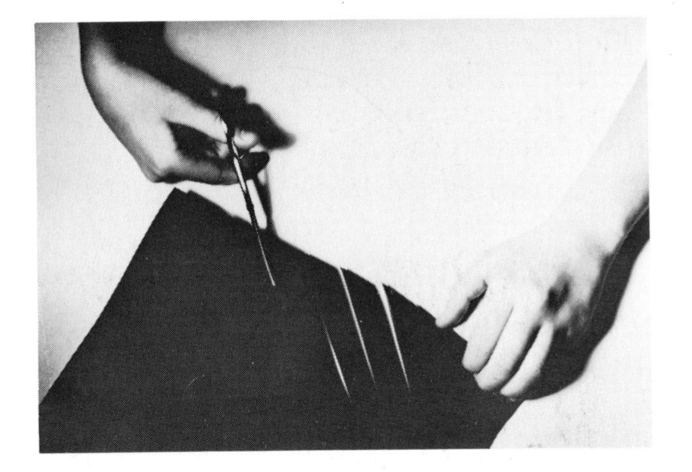

Illus. 25. Step 1.

Illus. 26. Step 2.

(Left)
Illus. 27. The completed stabile.

(Right)
Illus. 28. An asymmetrical design has been formed into a cylindrical shape. Zigzag strips, as well as strips of differing widths, make the design interesting. Notice that one vertical strip has been superimposed upon another.

Wastebaskets are very simple to make. Illus. 29 shows how a woven design can be pasted around circular cardboard or metal containers. You might make a smaller basket using an oatmeal box, salt container or cleanser box. Covered with paper-woven designs, these are useful as hair-curler boxes, yarn baskets, scrap boxes, carrying cases, pencil or brush holders. You can attach a cord to opposite sides of the carton as a handle.

Another approach to a woven three-dimensional basket is weaving right on the container itself, as shown in Illus. 30 and 31. The circular oatmeal box illustrates how you thread the carton with warp. Black paper strips, about 2 inches longer than the height of the oatmeal carton, are cut in ½-inch widths. Then place these vertical strips a little more than ½ inch apart so that the carton shows in between. Bend the top inch of each strip over the rim and paste to the inside. Do the same with the bottom inch. You are now ready to thread the weft, or horizontal strips.

The square, gallon-sized cardboard milk carton in Illus. 31 is threaded in the same way. The completed basket has light blue and pink paper strips of various widths woven in and out of the vertical black warp.

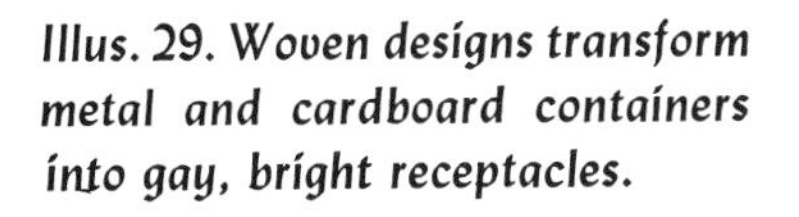

Illus. 29. Woven designs transform metal and cardboard containers into gay, bright receptacles.

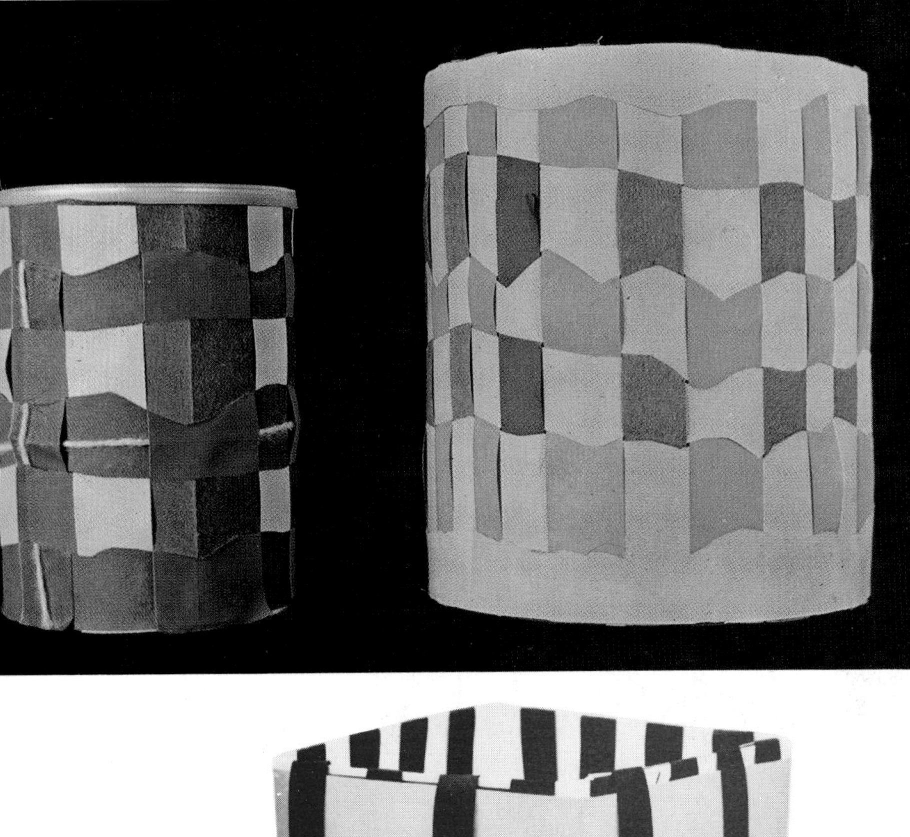

Illus. 30.

Illus. 31.

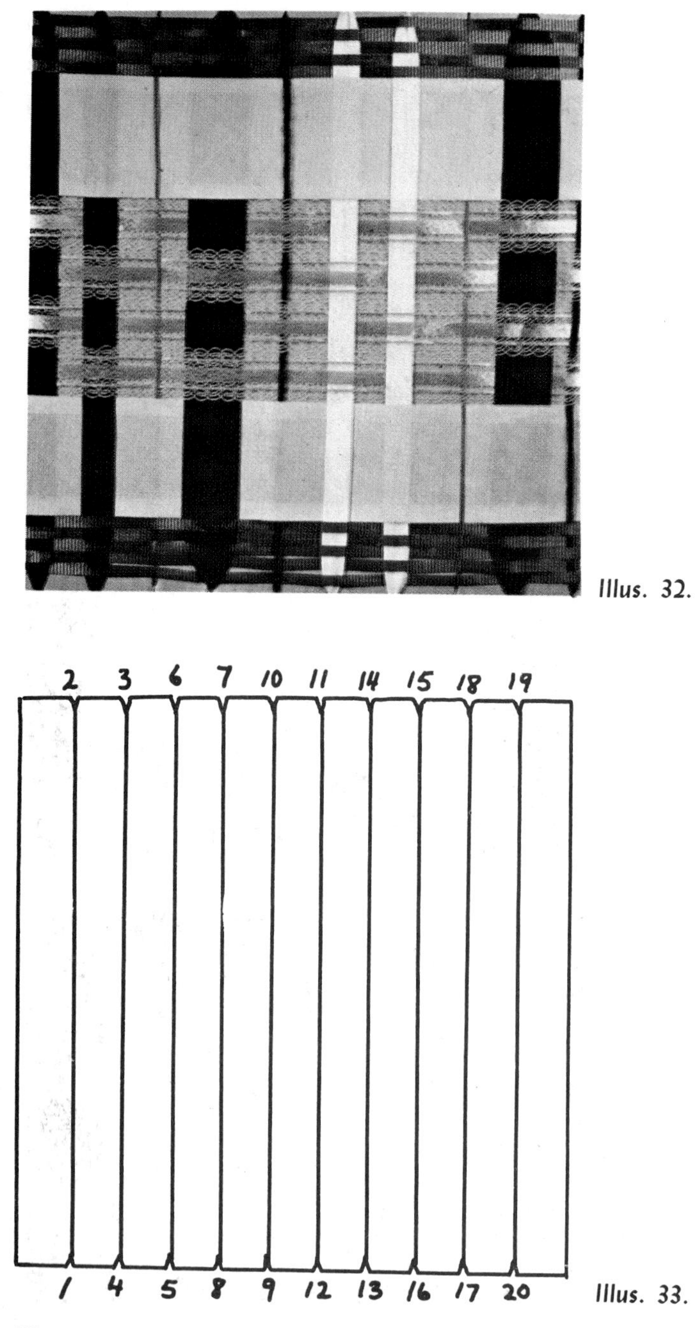

Illus. 32.

Illus. 33.

WEAVING ON A CARDBOARD LOOM

Illus. 32 shows the results you can get if you decide to weave on a corrugated cardboard loom. To thread this loom, cut evenly spaced notches, at least 1 inch apart, along the top and bottom edges of the cardboard loom. In our example, black yarn is used. Beginning at the lower left corner, insert the yarn into notch No. 1 (see Illus. 33). Pull the strand vertically across the surface of the loom towards the top rim and position in Notch No. 2.

Then, run the yarn across the reverse side of the loom and place into Notch No. 3, which lies one inch away from Notch No. 2, along the top rim. Next, pull the yarn strand downward across the loom's front surface and position into Notch No. 4, which is about 1 inch away from the bottom Notch No. 1. From the rear side of the loom, place the strand in Notch No. 5, which is the third notch over, bottom left. Continue the threading process until the vertical strands are secured by all of the top and bottom notches. Illus. 33 shows the threading procedure used to create our design.

The horizontal weft materials—red paper ribbon, gold satin ribbon and pink cloth—are woven in and out of the vertical warp. Wide black strips of ribbon are placed vertically and laced into the top and bottom notches. These ribbons cover the yarn warp—they are not a substitute for it.

You could create an open weave revealing the loom beneath if you use a piece of colored construction paper or metallic foil to cover the cardboard before you begin. In this way, the loom itself becomes part of the design.

DIFFERENT SHAPED LOOMS

So far your paper-woven articles have been created on a square or rectangular paper loom, but you can weave on looms which have been shaped to suggest recognizable objects. People, animals and holiday symbols can all be woven easily. You might make Halloween pumpkins and witches, Christmas angels, stars, bells and wreaths, Easter bunnies and lilies or Thanksgiving turkeys and pilgrims. Woven shapes representing holidays could serve as place mats at school and home parties or as centerpieces.

A boy's birthday party could be greatly enlivened by the sturdy cowboy in Illus 34. A white construction paper loom with slits of various widths allows for a variety of pattern from feet to hat. You can make good use of the classified ads from the newspapers in paper weaving—they add both texture and design. The hat contains vertical slits with horizontal strips of black construction paper and strips of classified newsprint. Wide jagged strips of ads are woven in a vertical direction to suggest patches in the trousers. A checkerboard shirt is a simple pattern to make by weaving black strips into vertical slits on the white construction paper.

Illus. 35 shows a pumpkin made entirely from construction paper. To make this symmetrical form, cut your pumpkin shape into a *folded* paper loom. Here black and white strips are woven into the vertical slits on an orange loom. Circular shapes of black construction paper serve as eyes that have triangular-shaped white eyeballs. Fringey eyelashes are simple to make in a number of ways—our pumpkin's lashes can be bent back at the ends to simulate curly ones, or straight back for a wide-eyed effect. A great new-moon mouth makes this pumpkin happy, but you can make a mouth that can convey any mood—straight for serious, curved down for sad.

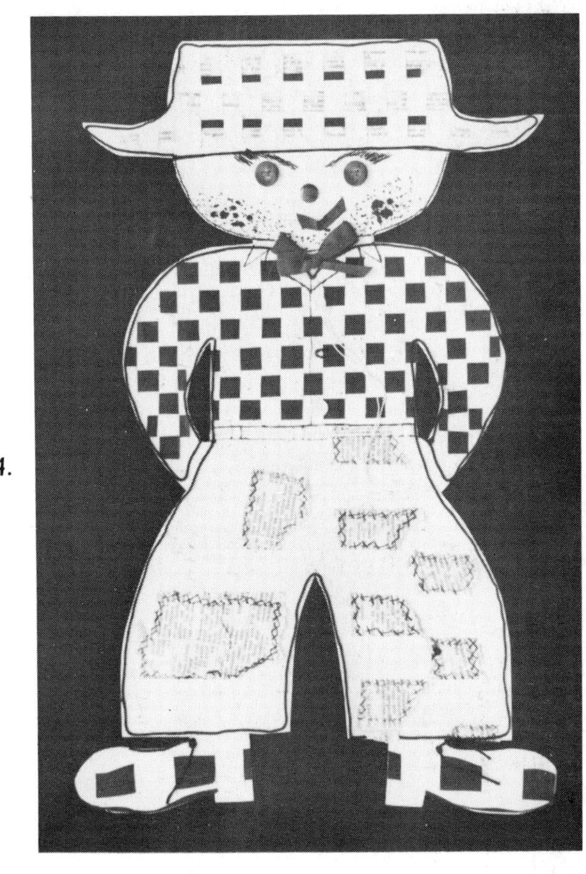

Illus. 34.

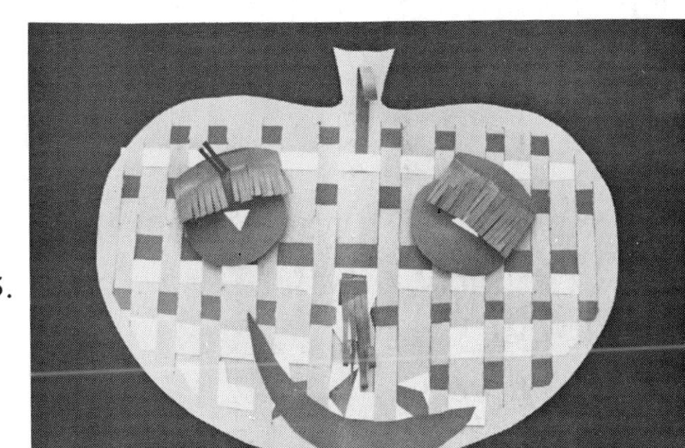

Illus. 35.

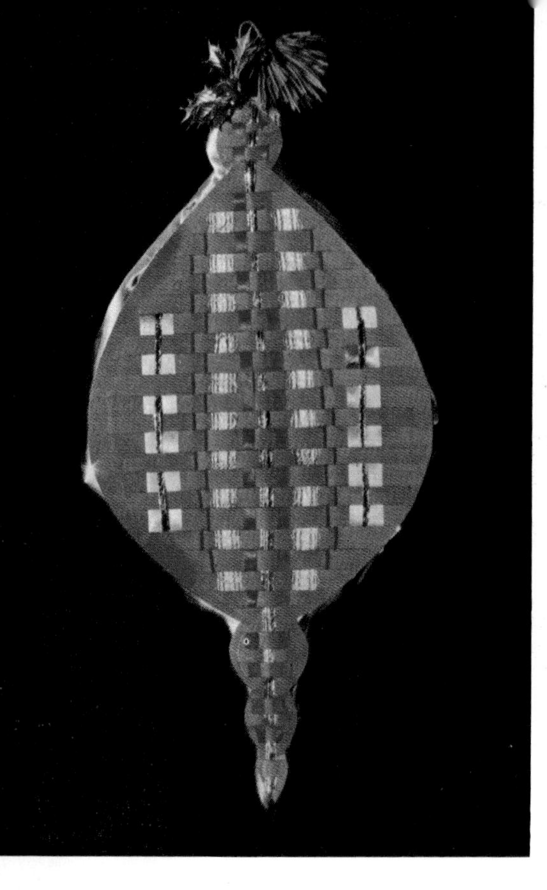

Illus. 36. A rich design on this ornament is made by weaving red satin, gold satin, gold lace and open-weave cellophane ribbons through red construction paper.

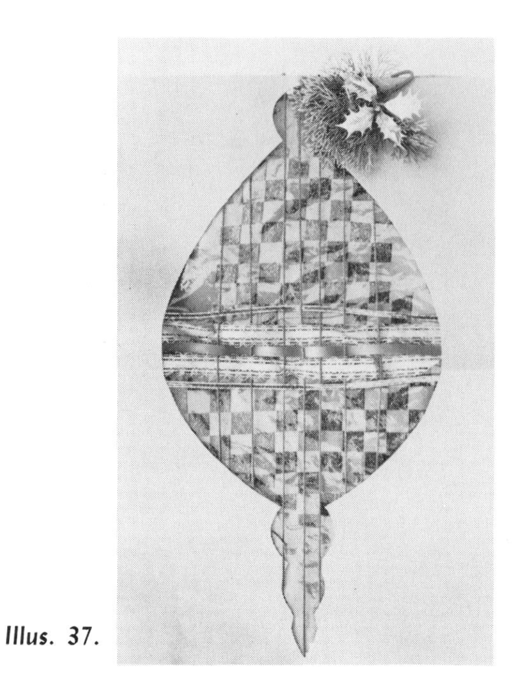

Illus. 37.

If you make a Christmas tree ornament like the one in Illus. 36, you can put the piece of construction paper that you cut the form from to good use. Illus. 37 shows the piece of red paper used as a border for another ornament, in which red strings are taped on the back side of the red paper and show through the large cut-out. Red ribbons and metallic ribbons are woven in and out of the red strings and are placed in the middle of the oval. Red cellophane covers the rear of the red sheet completely. Behind the red cellophane, white strips of paper and metallic strips of ribbon, all even in width, were woven together to create the checkerboard pattern.

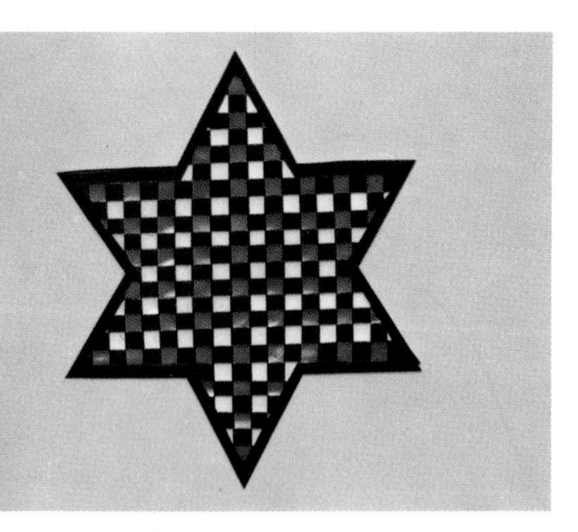

Illus. 38. A unique star can be set atop your Christmas tree if you weave red and white shiny strips of paper into a black loom.

Illus. 39. Tom Turkey, cut from black construction paper, is good enough to preside at the Thanksgiving table. Notice how the orange and yellow rectangles differ in direction and color scheme in each section to avoid monotony.

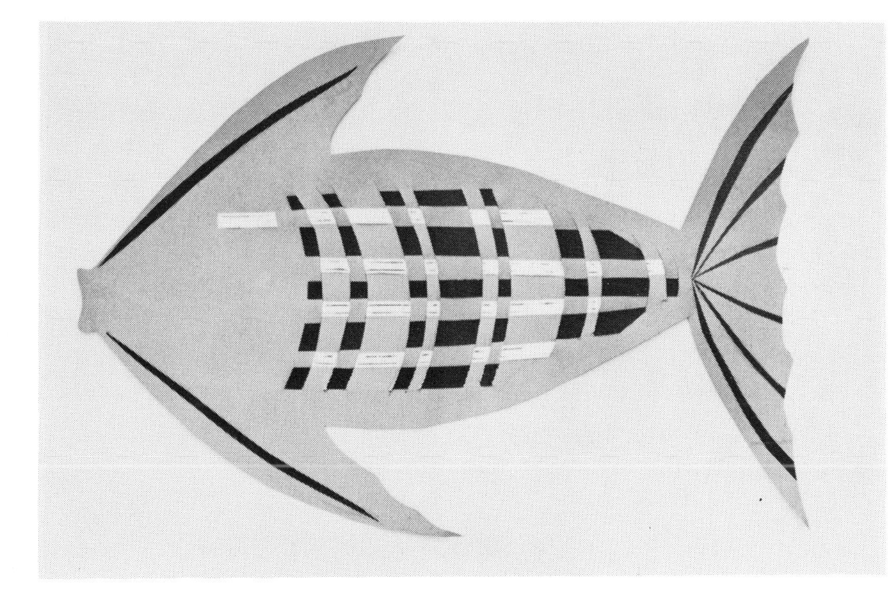

Illus. 40. A rare fish, achieved by cutting curved vertical slits and weaving black paper and silver ribbon across a dark blue paper loom. The blue paper was folded down the middle in order to get this symmetrical design. Strips of black paper grace the fins and tail.

Illus. 41.

For Thanksgiving you could make a gay rooster instead of a turkey, or decorate the Easter table with a hen and chicks. The rooster in Illus. 41 has a variety of woven patterns that add a great deal of interest. In addition, the materials used in each area differ, as do the widths of the slit spacings. Strips of red cellophane are woven in the tail section, and white paper strips and green cellophane in the central body section. Crushed, twisted strips of red cellophane add an interesting pattern and texture to the breast area. Narrow green and red cellophane strips woven into narrowly spaced slits in the head and a large sequin for an eye complete this big blue rooster. For Easter, traditional pastel colors might be used. A Fourth of July bird could be red, white and blue.

From the insect world you can make a big woven butterfly. The symmetry of the butterfly lends itself of course to a folded paper loom. You can make the body from a tightly rolled sheet of newspaper and cover it with a soft material like yarn. Hat pins or curler pins make satisfactory antennae and the edges of the wings can be decorated with little sequins or buttons of various shapes. Although the natural colors found in the butterfly are often striking, you could use colors that might never be found in nature, such as the brown construction paper wings and the chartreuse woven strips in the butterfly shown in Illus. 42.

Illus. 42.

Exploration with paper weaving will lead you to discover many weaving processes and paper materials, all of which will result in intriguing, aesthetic designs. Even though you may have to repeat shapes and patterns, you can easily avoid monotonous, unimaginative checkerboard effects.

2. Paper Window Transparencies

One of the most spectacular of the many possibilities in working in papercraft is making paper window transparencies. The lovely, richly colored stained glass windows which are the product of a vanishing art can be recreated in your own home or school simply and effectively.

Before you start on a paper window project you must remember that it will be two-dimensional. Do not select a design that requires depth to be effective. You might pay a visit to a church, synagogue, or public building such as a library or museum to see a real stained glass window. Many old houses have a stained glass window or two.

The medieval glazier started work on his window by drawing a cartoon (not a comic strip but a plan for the window's design). He made the cartoon in full size on a whitened table. Heavy dark lines were drawn upon this surface to indicate the window's iron and lead tracings. The tracings are the dark strips that hold the pieces of glass in place. Although they serve a functional purpose—providing strength—they add a very important aesthetic element—line. You will use tracings to determine the composition of your designs.

Keeping in mind that most parts of the windows will be transparent, or partially so, decide on what kinds of papers you can use. Since the tracings are dark and heavy, black construction paper is a good base to work on. Cellophane of various colors and tissue paper are possible choices for the glass.

Illus. 43. This brilliant stained-glass window is made of paper! Colored construction paper, tissue papers and cellophanes were used to produce a religious motif which simulates many of the fine windows found in Gothic cathedrals. When placed in a clear glass window such as this, the effect of the strong light from outside produces rich glowing colors.

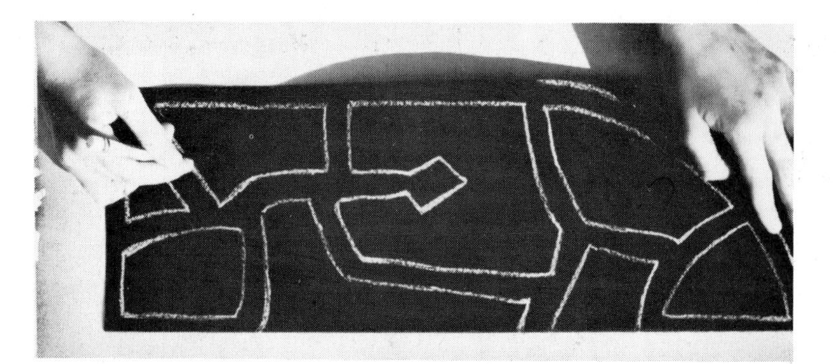

Illus. 44.

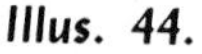

Illus. 45.

Illus. 46

Fold the sheet of construction paper parallel to the longest side. Using pencil or white crayon, lay out the plan of your design in the manner shown in Illus. 44. You can vary the size of your windows by joining several sheets of paper together. Two sheets wide and four sheets high make a tall narrow window as in a Gothic cathedral. To join the pieces, place masking tape along the joining edges on the reverse side.

Next, keeping the paper folded, cut out the negative shapes, leaving only the tracings (Illus. 45). It is a good idea to unfold the paper now and then to see if you can make any improvements in the design.

When you have a complete cut-out with just the tracings left, you can start cutting out your brightly colored tissue or cellophane paper. First, place the tissue beneath the openings of the window. Trace the cut-out shapes and then cut them out slightly larger than the tracing so as to leave room for overlapping the tissue across the *reverse* side of the tracing (Illus. 46). Elmer's glue or library paste are both satisfactory binders.

As your design will be symmetrical, you might also balance your colors in the same way—each corresponding area with the same color. You should experiment with the colored papers to see the variety of effects that can be achieved. For instance, red on red produces a deeper red, red on yellow produces orange. Or you might use a small piece of another color here and there. In some areas, crossed strips of tissue paper could create patterns within the shapes. Opaque shapes of construction paper serve

Illus. 47. This schoolroom is flooded with color when the sun pours through the paper window transparencies. Before making these designs, the students tested the effects of their colored papers, separately and combined, against the window. Notice the simplicity of these designs.

Illus. 48. Here is an example of the effectiveness of both large shapes and small shapes. You need not necessarily make a complicated design in order to produce an impressive window transparency.

well as small accents when pasted over the transparent areas of color.

Since it is light that produces the most striking aspect of stained glass windows, you will want to mount your design on either a window which receives sunlight or indoors on a glass surface that has light behind it. If a window or glass is not available, try mounting it on a light-colored wall, but first face the transparency on the reverse side with white paper.

While religious subjects are traditional for stained glass, you need not be restricted to them—non-representational designs can be created either in conjunction with the traditional or on their own.

Illus. 49. This modernistic yet religious paper transparent window displays the use of broad masses of color and design. In spite of the repetition of the cross throughout, variety was achieved.

Illus. 50. A more delicately executed design but still simple. Notice here that although the shapes on each side correspond exactly, the colors do not, giving this perfectly balanced window an interest it might not have had.

OTHER METHODS FOR MAKING WINDOW TRANSPARENCIES

Illus. 51. Another method of making paper-window transparencies is by the wax-paper technique, in which the materials are fused together between pieces of wax paper. Here, yarn and colored tissue papers have been fused to make an attractive window for a child's room.

Illus. 51 was accomplished by using the "wax-paper technique." Here you will use a hot iron to fuse all of the materials together. In Illus. 51, a design composed of yarn and colored tissue paper cut-outs was placed between two sheets of wax paper. When applying a hot iron to the surfaces of your wax-paper window, it is best not to use a back-and-forth movement. The iron tends to tear the wax paper when it glides over the raised strands of yarn positioned between the two wax-paper surfaces. Place the iron down, lift it, and place down in another area. Continue this procedure until you have completely covered the surface.

String or yarn can play an important role in these paper transparencies. They serve as tracings either to outline shapes or add accents where there are vague areas of color.

When using the wax-paper technique you might want to block out certain areas with opaque materials. Repeated opaque shapes add interest to a window design when juxtaposed with transparent areas of tissue paper, cellophane paper or clear wax paper. You can use black construction paper to fill shapes formed by string or other lines. Or India ink or a mixture of black tempera paint and hand soap might cover the resisting wax-paper surfaces when painted over certain areas.

Illus. 52 (on the next page) shows another im-

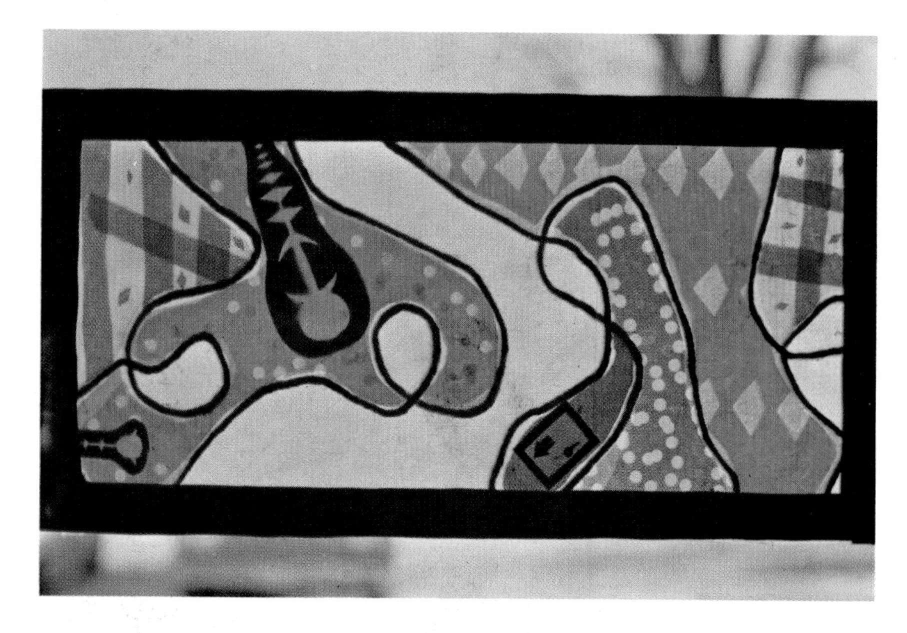

Illus. 52. Another wax-paper window transparency that shows considerable thought. The tissue paper shapes were cut after the yarn was laid down. Then the paper was carefully placed within the outlines and they were fused together. Compare this with the random placement of the yarn in Illus. 53.

aginative paper window transparency. Tissue paper shapes are cut carefully to fit the areas defined by black yarn and are fused, as before, between two sheets of wax paper.

A paper punch was used to make the small circular shapes in the central orange area. Narrow orange tissue paper strips form a design on yellow tissue on both sides. Notice the balance of color these two varying shapes provide. To make the diamond-shaped pattern in the green area, the tissue paper must be folded back and forth like an Oriental fan. With a scissors, V-shapes are removed alternately from both sides of the fan. When the fan is unfolded the pattern emerges. The piece of black construction paper, cut larger than the tissues, forms a wide border which defines the edges and serves to repeat the black color of the yarn tracings.

The window in Illus. 53 reveals an even freer approach to abstract design. Here the yarn does not

Illus. 53.

entirely serve as a definition of shape, but does unify the various elements of the design. To achieve this, the yarn is placed upon the wax-paper surfaces *after* the tissue paper and construction papers are arranged.

Illus. 55 shows a stylized Christmas tree. While this one is composed of squares, you might make one of any number of shapes. These black construction paper squares were folded once into halves or twice into quarters. Then while still folded, interesting shapes were cut into them, both along the edges and on the inner part. The narrow bands of black which were left serve as tracings. Between the tracings, colored pieces of tissue are pasted. Notice how well balanced the colors are in these small patterns. This design is loose and simply pasted on to the window. However, you could, as in Illus. 54, join them by yarn and make a window mobile.

Illus. 55.

Illus. 54.

During the Christmas season you might want to make some holiday symbols for your windows. There are many projects besides stained glass transparencies. All kinds of forms from Santa Claus to snowflakes are possible. Our window in Illus. 54 shows some ornamental shapes suggesting stars, snowflakes and Christmas tree ornaments. As you can see, these are symmetrical forms, so start by *folding* a sheet of black construction paper. Cut out your shapes and then unfold the paper and paste colored tissue on the reverse sides to fill the openings. You can attach many ornaments together by stapling them on to a long strand of yarn and hanging them from the pieces of wood between the window panes.

Illus. 56. This little lady, ready for an evening out, is wearing an outfit made from newsprint rubbed over a plastic doily with crayon (see page 34, crayon-relief technique).

3. Paper Collage and Montage

Collage and montage are two popular art forms in painting, photography and in papercraft that grew up during the first half of the 20th century. The French word, "collage," meaning a pasting of paper, refers to the application of a wide variety of materials—including pieces of paper, newspaper and illustrations—on to a heavy background such as an oil painting—or in our case, cardboard. Any number of elements might be incorporated into an artist's collage; including pebbles, cloth, wood, beads, wire, etc., and all are designed to provide *texture*. Because of the tactile nature of collage, it might be called a "texture picture." So, when planning your collages, you must appeal to both sight and touch.

"Montage," meaning in French a putting together, while similar to collage, restricts the artist in his choice of materials. Montage is composed of photographic images, blended together. They can be cut up, separated and then united in such a way that the original subjects are not recognizable. Montage then relies entirely on a visual appeal.

COLLAGE FIGURES

Imaginative collage figures are fun to make and you will find that often the color or textural quality of whatever paper materials you have at hand will determine the nature of your figure. Paper doilies might suggest a delicate princess, or a sheet of dark brown construction paper a dark-skinned jungle warrior as in Illus. 57. Tinfoil earrings and a scrap piece of fringe cord decorate our king of the jungle, but you might add a clothespin nose, wire bracelets, steel wool hair or any other odd bits of things you have handy.

Drab grey and green construction paper suggested the basis for the hobo in Illus. 58. Broken, vari-colored buttons close his jacket, odd pieces of cloth make pockets and patches and a piece of string holds up his ragged trousers. Imagine all the realistic items you could add to your hobo—safety pins, band-aids, whiskers. What will make a good hobo bag?

Illus. 57.

Illus. 58.

CRAYON RELIEF TECHNIQUE

Probably every child has at one time made a "rubbing" of a coin, using a pencil and thin paper. In much the same way you can create your own textures and patterns on paper in making a collage. Newsprint is an ideal paper for this technique because it is both thin and smooth. Peel colored crayons all the way down so that one whole long side can be used for rubbing.

Many coarse materials and surfaces are suitable for the crayon-relief technique: placemats, screens, fly swatters, vegetable graters, burlap, sandpaper.

When you have chosen your colors and textural material, place separate sheets of newsprint over each piece of texture. Hold the paper as close to the material as possible and, with even strokes, using the side of the crayon, rub the paper until the entire pattern is both visible and slightly raised above the smooth surface.

The flower blossoms in Illus. 59 were created from a number of objects with interesting surfaces. Sheets of newsprint were crayon-rubbed over a brick wall, a cut-glass dish, corrugated cardboard, and a waffle iron, so that each flower has a different texture and color.

A plastic doily, the grill of a furnace filter and paper backing from tiles, when rubbed by colored crayons on newsprint, produced the effects in Illus. 60.

Illus. 59.

Illus. 60.

TISSUE PAPER

A wonderfully versatile paper for collage is tissue paper. You can appliqué colorful shapes on to a white or other light-colored background paper, cardboard or painted plywood and masonite. Liquid starch, diluted Elmer's glue, liquid floor wax or shellac can be used to join layers of tissue to the backing. As you learned in Chapter 2 when making paper window transparencies, surprising things begin to happen when you overlap layers of tissue—new colors and shades appear. This can be seen very well in Illus. 61, where a few basic colors have produced a wide variety of hues. Notice, too, how the overlapping of the triangular forms has resulted in a multitude of different-sized as well as different-colored triangles.

Using liquid floor wax as an adhesive, when done very carefully, causes tissue paper colors to run, or bleed, and results in a striking effect. You can also take a single sheet of tissue, dip it into floor wax, lay it carefully over your completed collage and let the color run off on to the surface. When you have achieved the right degree of color, remove the tissue. Try placing several smaller pieces of wax-wet tissue of varying colors in different parts of your collage and instead of removing them, allow them to remain as part of the design. Bleeding edges can be emphasized and outlined by India ink or fine yarn.

Illus. 61. An ethereal effect is attained by overlaying different-colored tissue paper.

Illus. 62. Tissue cut with pinking shears, and varying shades of pink and purple, give this design a softer feeling. The leaves and yarn provide a good contrast. Yarn may be placed between the layers of tissue or upon the top surface.

CONSTRUCTION PAPER

Even if you limit yourself to the use of construction paper in composing a collage, you can add variety by using different colors and shapes, such as in Illus. 65, which is made entirely from construction paper of different shades. The theme of musical notes and symbols provides an interesting array of shapes.

Another construction paper collage is shown in Illus. 64. This imaginative bird shows a nice unity of color in the use of grey, chartreuse, orange and black. Notice how the edges of some of the shapes are torn slightly, forming a contrast with the other clean-cut parts.

MAGAZINE PATTERNS

Magazines offer an excellent source of texture and color for both the collage and montage techniques. When making a collage, you must consider the color of the background paper in relation to the

Illus. 64. This asymmetrical, many-colored bird can be looked at horizontally and upside down also.

Illus. 65. Musical symbols cut from construction paper make a gay assemblage of shapes.

Illus. 66. An owl solemnly introduces a Halloween theme of cats, witches, bats, etc. Construction paper, wall paper and magazine pictures combine to give the eerie effect.

magazine colors you choose. Of course, sometimes you will completely cover the background, but you may also want to work it in as part of the pattern. Plain open areas can offer an interesting contrast to busy textures. However, select your magazine papers before deciding on the background.

An excellent adhesive for magazine paper is rubber cement. You will find that the slick papers you are using will not buckle up as they might with other joining substances.

The mosaic-like collage in Illus. 67 is composed of torn shapes taken from magazines and pasted on to a sheet of white paper. The white background provides a relief for the surrounding irregular areas of pattern and color. Pen with India ink is used to accent the torn edges and to emphasize the patterns, as well as to create a feeling of texture. Notice the harmony of color in this collage.

Illus. 67. An abstract pattern, offering variety in color, shape and texture. Brushing with India ink (no water) produces the rough black on white areas.

Illus. 68. A musical theme, with a conductor, piano, notes, and a baton-waving hand. The baton is a tightly rolled paper which is advertising records, and the piano keys, of various colors and textures, were gathered from different magazines.

Illus. 69. These magazine patterns have been gathered into an abstract design, but an ocean floor is suggested by floating plants and leaning shells.

Illus. 70. Leaves whirl to give a fall theme. Some of the shapes are outlined with India ink, and ink patterns form the background of the framed picture.

Illus. 71. A collage filled with uncommon shapes, joined by ink lines.

Illus. 72. Pen and ink patterns, each slightly varied to prevent monotony, unite these tumbling shapes.

Illus. 73. Pen and ink are used to create the white waves of the foreground. Through the holes they create the eye is drawn to skies and seas of misty blue-green colors.

Illus. 74. A clown dominates the scene as tents and performers express the gaiety of the circus.

Illus. 75. A large egg, made with yarn and ink, contains paper eggs inside it. The chocolate people in front have been decorated with ears to suggest bunnies; we will let you guess the theme!

Illus. 76. Here is a crazy-quilt pattern, with an emphasis on horizontal and vertical lines. Pen and ink designs fill in gaps between pictures, and highlight some of them.

Illus. 77. Paper shapes were cut and gathered into a floral arrangement. Notice how balanced the blues and reds are.

Illus. 78.

The plant world forms the theme for both Illus. 77 and 78. In Illus. 78 a sheet of orange construction paper forms the background and dominant color for the entire collage. The three large blossoms are composed of petals cut from different-colored magazine patterns. The background space is divided into a variety of geometric shapes by India ink lines, painted on with a brush. Note how well these shapes complement the flower outlines. Dot and line patterns move in a variety of directions, tending to stabilize the fluid movement of the design. The blue of the border and landscape tends to "cool off" the warm orange background.

When creating a montage, magazines as well as newspapers and snapshots provide an abundance of photographic material. If you wish, you might select a specific theme and then hunt for all possible subjects relating to the central idea. Or you can simply select your photographs for an over-all compositional or color effect without a special subject. For instance, a tree cut from a magazine might be used in part only to give a textural effect or photographed grass might represent a fabric. Rug or linoleum patterns could in turn suggest objects in nature.

The theme of childhood was used in the montage in Illus 80. Many of the experiences of the early years of life are recalled here and the total effect is rather dreamlike. In the upper left corner two children stroll through a lacy forest with a parent. In the bottom left corner, a boy clasps a newborn duckling as a mother on the upper right holds an infant in her palm. The rapt attention of the group of children in the middle symbolizes one of childhood's most popular activities—listening to stories.

Suggestions for mounting your collages and montages can be found on page 48 in Chapter 4.

Illus. 79. Eggs, lemons and oranges juxtaposed against the sea, mountains, castle, and river make a bizarre composition.

Illus. 80. Childhood is the theme of this montage and is expressed here by loving, listening and looking—all vital to a child.

Illus. 81. This paper mosaic is made of pieces of colored construction paper which were pasted on to a large sheet of grey construction paper. Notice how the large plain areas surrounding the Madonna and the simplicity of her face provide a pleasing and restful contrast to the busy patterns of the paper tesserae. The strips radiating from the Mother and Child are made of tinfoil.

4. Paper Mosaics

Your first attempts at making mosaics from paper can lead you into one of the most exciting and creative aspects of paper crafting.

An infinite variety of papers are well suited to mosaics—construction paper, poster paper, metallic foil, colored tissue, Japanese papers, tagboard, magazine paper, cellophane, gift wrapping paper, newsprint, paper towels and napkins, cardboard, stationery, sandpaper and wallpaper.

The objects and forms of a mosaic have sharp edges. Color areas are abrupt in their transition from light to dark values. Shading of objects can only be suggested, as subtle transitions from light to dark are difficult to achieve. Consequently, the artist is limited in his ability to realize great depth in space or roundness of form. The greatest excitement of the mosaic technique lies in the broad masses of color and glowing deep tones provided by the paper materials.

When planning a paper mosaic, you might want to draw a cartoon which will outline the mosaic's *broad* areas of color. The finished cartoon can be transferred on to the mosaic's background which might be made of paper, masonite, plywood, fibreboard, etc. The cartoon should be kept simple—it is the paper *tesserae* that make the composition as detailed as you want.

The term *tessera* is derived from the Latin, and means "small piece." The early Christian and Byzantine mosaics were composed of numerous tesserae, cut from tile, glass or clay, and set in cement. The cracks in between were filled with grout.

Paper tesserae may be cut with a scissors or a

Illus. 82. Two tissue paper balloons, outlined in yarn, rise above the buildings of magazine paper and tinfoil, while two tinfoil ducks fly through the tissue paper sky. Notice how well the yellow border brings out the small yellow touches throughout and unifies the composition.

Illus. 83. You might start your mosaic by cutting, with scissors, a wide variety of shapes from a sheet of gold foil and from pieces of folded construction paper of different colors. In order to lay the tesserae down, cover the area of the design with glue. You will notice here that the general outlines of the mosaic have been laid out as a cartoon.

Illus. 84. Our finished mosaic is a non-representational design and shows a radial balance, that is, all the color and shapes seem to move outward from a central focal point. The various patterns and sizes of the tesserae show a harmony of both color and shape. Little accents are repeated throughout.

Illus. 85. A sheet of Japanese Shibui rice paper, placed over green construction paper, makes an appropriate web-like background for this spider mosaic. The dullness of the background serves to emphasize the richness of the body and the brilliance of the tinfoil legs. Black yarn outlines the insect's body and emphasizes the web-like character of the rice paper.

paper cutter. Interesting effects can also be achieved when papers are freely torn into bits. Both cut and torn shapes might be used in a single mosaic. The paper bits can either overlap or you can leave evenly spaced open areas between to suggest the cement or group of the original mosaics.

One of the most important characteristics of an aesthetically pleasing mosaic is contrast. By this time, you have learned many of the important aspects of paper crafting such as how to achieve variety by the use of color and shape and texture. You can put them to good use in making mosaics.

You might make a mosaic consisting entirely of cool colors such as blues and greens, along with varying shades of those two colors, placed against a white background. Or, you could use these same colors against a warm-colored background such as gold or red. Before you begin, decide on the overall impression you want to convey. Separate forms are most clearly seen when there is a sharp delineation between them—light against dark, warm against cool, rough against smooth, opaque against transparent, etc. A mosaic is especially suited to overlaying of tissue paper and cellophane to achieve a variance of color.

Illus. 86. A rare butterfly, constructed of colored tissue paper tesserae, hops from one leaf to another. This tissue paper mosaic was mounted on a piece of tagboard.

Illus. 87. This paper mosaic shows a multitude of patterns. In spite of this, the ship stands out immediately. Long, narrow paper strips suggest a calm sea under a threatening sky of squares and rectangles. Newspaper-ad tesserae provide an arresting pattern for the lower decks of the ship, hinting of the life and activity aboard. Notice how well balanced the lights and darks are in the whole composition.

A frame or border can add a great deal to your collage or mosaic, and you should use care in selecting it. Choose colors and materials that complement the design. A good frame provides a natural transition from the composition to its surroundings; therefore it must not in any way "fight" the design. Generally speaking, neutral colors, such as black, grey, or white are preferable. However, you must consider that if the design has weak colors, a strong-colored frame would overpower it. In the same way, a vibrantly colored mosaic might appear to pour over the edges of a weak-colored frame. When your design colors are strong, an in-between frame or mat might be best—one that picks up a medium-strong color within the composition.

However, you may wish to accent the dominant color—in which case you might use it in the frame, or there may be a "recessive" color—one that is used sparingly—that you wish to bring out. In any event, the best test for a suitable frame is to place next to the design, one at a time, a variety of colors. In this way, you can get an idea of the final effect. Illus. 86 (see also Illus. 1) shows how well the use of a double border can increase the impact of both the dominant and restricted colors within the composition. Notice, however, that the inner border is much narrower than the outer one.

If your design is non-representational, and you feel that it can be displayed in a number of ways—vertically, horizontally, or upside down, you will want your border to have all four sides of even width. However, if not, there is one interesting point worth mentioning concerning the sides of a frame. When a frame is on a wall, the bottom appears to be narrower than the top. Therefore, you can, if you

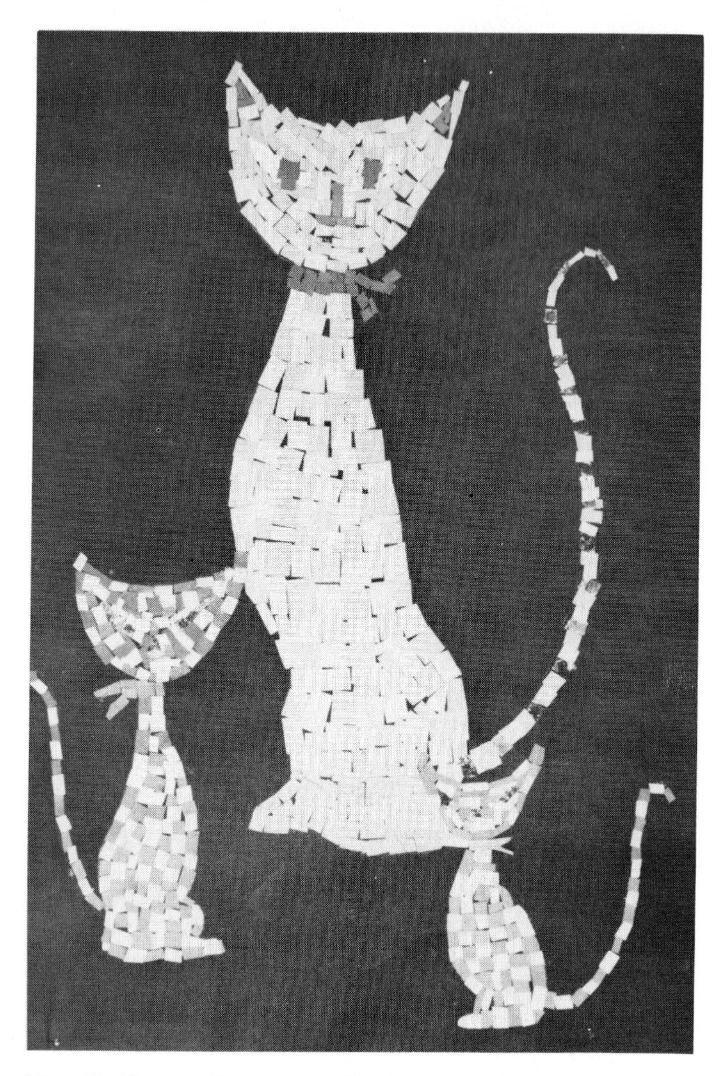

Illus. 88. Three calico cats, made of construction paper tesserae, peer out of tinfoil eyes from a black construction paper background.

Illus. 89. An exuberant mosaic clown appears about to be pulled up into the sky by his paper balloons.

wish, make the bottom part of your frame slightly wider to offset this visual imbalance.

In most cases, collages, montages and mosaics are simply pasted over one or two or more sheets of construction paper which then serve as the frame, with Elmer's glue providing a lasting adhesive. Or you can mount them in the same way on a thin sheet of plywood, cut slightly larger than the design. Using wood stain, or shoe polish, you can give the plywood a finished look. Another simple material is masonite, which you can paint with enamel or acrylics. Sheets of cork are available from many arts and crafts stores and can be used in conjunction with other materials to make a double frame. For a small composition that might require support, tagboard, being stiff, might be a suitable framing material.

For a more professional-looking frame, a 14-ply mat board, available in white, black, grey, as well as warmer colors, can be used.

With an X-acto knife, or another very sharp cutting instrument, cut the mat board to required height and width, after having decided on the width of the frame. This width should correlate well with the composition—it should be neither too heavy nor too skimpy.

Next, place your design against the reverse side of the mat board and lightly sketch its outline. Then remove it and make a ruled outline at least ¼ inch *smaller* than the sketch.

Now cut a window through the mat board, carefully following your outline. Place your composition against the reverse of the board so that it shows through. Using gummed paper tape, secure it to the back side of the board. In order to avoid future warpage, run the tape on each side so that it ends a short distance from the corners.

The finished mat board can be given extra stability by glueing a piece of corrugated cardboard to the reverse. The cardboard should be cut slightly smaller than the board. Place a narrow band of glue about 1 inch from the outer edges of the board. Be sure not to touch the composition with the glue or it will cause it to wrinkle up.

The finished mat board can be placed into a thin wooden or metal frame. In this case, corrugated cardboard would not be necessary. Often these frames have their own cardboard backing, which you might glue lightly to the sides of the mat board.

A three-dimensional frame, simple to make and very inexpensive, can be constructed from corrugated cardboard. Illus. 94 shows the procedure for making this frame. The inner rectangle marked "A"

Illus. 90 (Above). This parrot is composed of unique tesserae—the color charts of a paint dealer, which allows the delicate shading on, for example, the breast. The tesserae are set on a piece of blue construction paper. This is a very carefully planned design.

Illus. 91 (Left). Magazine paper and construction paper form a proud rooster. The small squares scattered throughout the plain background and the border could repeat and balance the restricted colors in the rooster. For instance, you would probably give him a red wattle or a yellow beak, and these colors would make good balancing spots elsewhere.

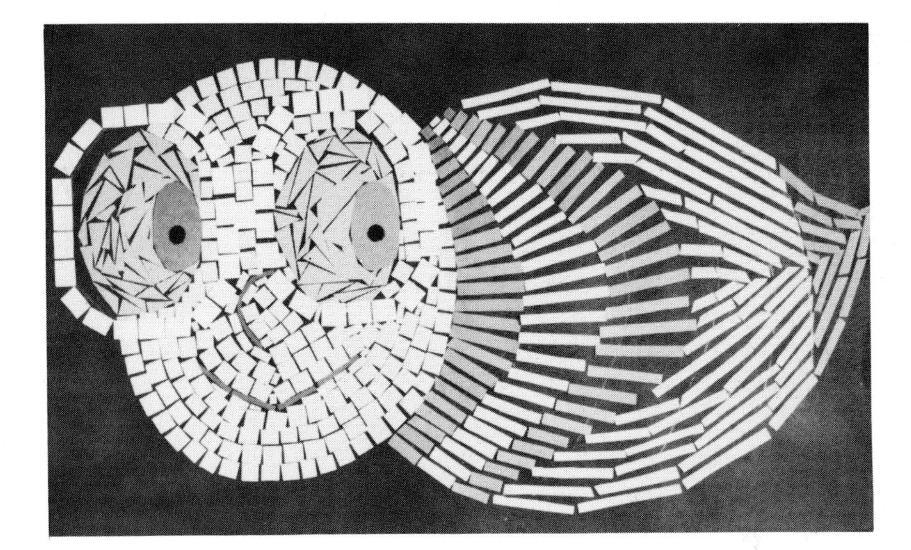

Illus. 92. Variety of shape—squares, rectangles, triangles, and circles—lends interest to a sleek bumblebee mosaic.

is the exact area of the mosaic or collage. Outline this area in pencil on a large piece of cardboard.

Since your cardboard must be larger than this, allow, let us say, 2 inches for the frame, and make another outline 2 inches larger. The corners of this rectangle are marked "C" in the illustration. Select a point a short distance from the first "C" corner and mark it "B." Measure exactly the same distance in the other direction and mark that "B." Do this for all four corners. The distance should be exactly equal in each place. Draw a light pencil line from these "B" points to the corners of the rectangle "A," as shown in the drawing. The length of the "B"-"C" line will determine whether your frame is shallow or deep. The closer to "C" that "B" is, the shallower, and the farther away, the wider, your frame will be.

With a sharp knife, cut along the drawn "B" lines to the corners of "A." Remove these triangular pieces. Now with the knife, score (see page 56), not cut, along the four sides of rectangle "A." This will allow the cardboard to bend so that the edges marked "B" can touch one another. Using gummed paper tape, join the "B" edges together from the rear side, along all four corners. You now have a three-dimensional frame.

Before pasting your composition into place, you will undoubtedly want to decorate the cardboard frame. Crumpled tissue paper is an unusual covering.

Cut four strips of white tissue paper to dimensions which are slightly wider and longer than each of the four borders of your three-dimensional cardboard frame. Crinkle them up in your hands. Then slightly smooth out the many creases and paste the tissue strips over the four borders, using white library paste.

Bend the tissue over the outside edges of the frame.

Choose a suitable color tempera and paint the tissue. Be sure you brush color into all the recesses and raised areas. When dry, paint over the tissue with a slightly deeper shade of the same color. Use light brush strokes when applying the second coat

Illus. 93. A jack-in-the-box composed of a variety of paper tesserae—construction paper, cardboard, magazine paper, and the corrugated paper used as dividers in cookie boxes. Notice how the less-defined area of the spiral is emphasized by black yarn outlines.

so that the color touches only the raised areas of the crumpled paper. When the second color is dry, you could sprinkle metallic dust over the surface if you want.

Natural or colored burlap makes a nice covering for this kind of frame. Cut the burlap about 2 inches larger along all four sides than the frame. Soak the burlap in diluted Elmer's glue and leave it there long enough for it to become slightly tacky. During the tacky stage, place the burlap over the frame and press it against the cardboard surface. The soaked burlap will easily adhere to the frame, whereas it will not if dry and simply pasted on.

There are innumerable ways you might want to decorate the cardboard frame. Try to think of what materials or designs would be most effective with the composition.

You can either paste your design over the rectangle "A" or you might make a window so that it will show through. The nature of your work will probably determine the best means of showing it off.

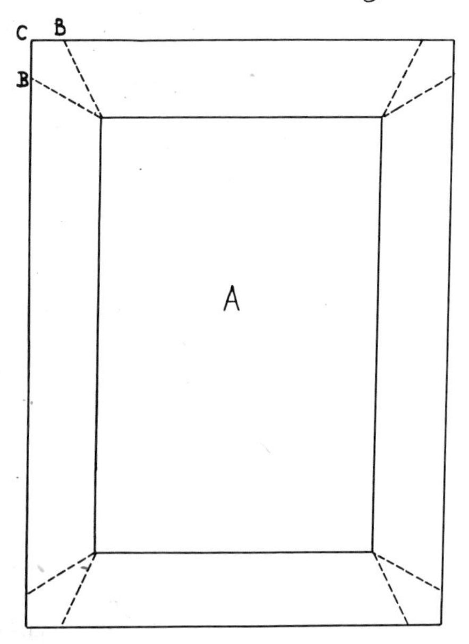

Illus. 94. Here is a simple three-dimensional cardboard frame you can use to mount not only your mosaics, but collages and montages, too. From one large piece of cardboard you can—by making the few incisions indicated by the dotted lines, folding the resulting edges over, cutting out the large retcangle "A" which is the outline of your composition—have a recessed frame. Decorate it with tissue paper, burlap, or paint.

Illus. 95. A wallpaper sample book provided this rooster with a wonderful variety of color and texture.

PART II: PAPER IN THE THIRD DIMENSION

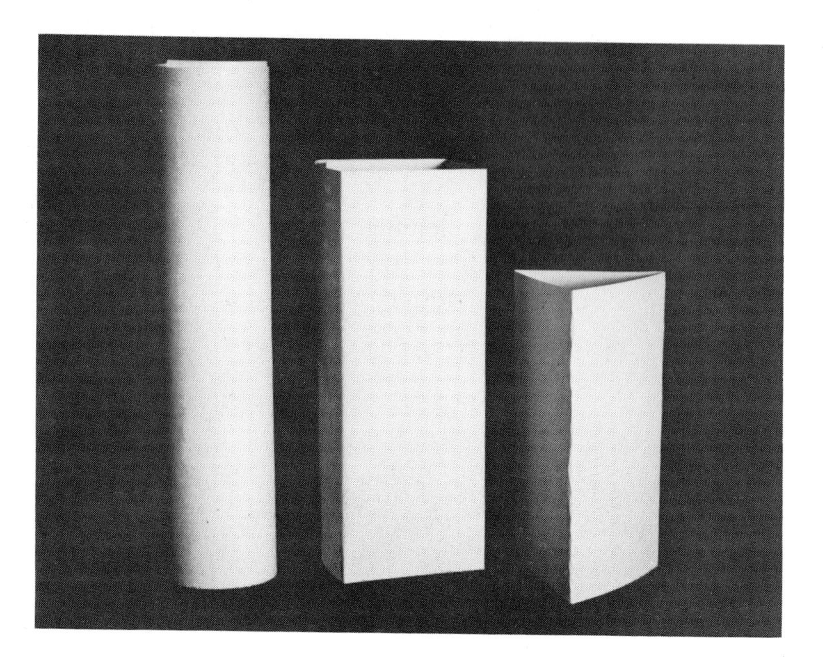

Illus. 96. A cylinder, a cube and a triangle—shapes which are basic to three-dimensional forms.

5. Basic Materials, Shapes and Suggestions for Paper Sculpture

You are now ready to add a new dimension to your paper crafting. However, you have probably, without realizing it, made a three-dimensional paper object in the form of a folded paper hat, sailboat or gliding airplane. You were practicing an art form that has existed for centuries—*origami*, or paper folding, which originated in the Orient. Now in our three-dimensional projects we will go beyond simple paper folding and include cutting, tearing, joining, twisting, and curling, and adding decorations.

Before you begin your paper sculpture there are many basic materials, shapes and techniques you should know and practice.

PAPER SELECTION

Illus. 97 shows many of the paper materials that you will find useful in three-dimensional sculpture. You should try to become a "collector" of paper. Whenever you come across an unusual piece of paper, set it aside. Try to find large quantities of paper of a single color and a single texture so that you will have an ample supply at hand and can cut each into smaller pieces if necessary. You could store papers of a similar nature in labelled boxes, such as smooth, rough, patterned, translucent, transparent, opaque, etc. In addition, these could be broken down into color groups.

The experience of collecting alone will increase your awareness of the infinite variety of textures and colors that are available around you every day.

CREATING GEOMETRIC FORMS

Once you have a good selection of papers, you should experiment with the construction of a few basic geometric, three-dimensional forms. The cylinder, cube and triangle shown in Illus. 96 are simple to make and will form, singly and combined, the basis for many of your sculptured objects.

To make the cylinder shown at the left in Illus. 96, a form especially useful for arms and legs of people and animals, join or overlap opposite ends of a rectangular sheet of paper. Secure the ends with staples, tape, or paper clips.

To make the cube shape in the middle of Illus. 96, take a rectangular sheet of paper, fold it in half in either direction, then fold it in half again in the same direction. You should have three creases. Unfold, and form the cube. Fasten together on each end. If you fold the paper in half the long way, you will have a long narrow cube shape. If you fold it the short way, you will have a boxier cube. Using a square piece of paper, you will end up with a perfect square. Try making as many different lengths and sizes as possible—even very tiny ones, as they will come in handy many times.

The three-dimensional triangle at the right in Illus. 96 is made by again taking a rectangular sheet of paper, but this time fold it the way you would a business letter—that is, folding both ends towards each other and then overlapping one with the other, so that you end up with two creases dividing the paper into three equal sections. Then unfold and fasten together as before.

You should practice these basic forms on as many different kinds of paper as possible. Each may react differently to being folded and also to the kind

Illus. 97. Collecting many kinds of paper will enable you to make objects which are rich in contrast. Shown here are (1) crepe paper, (2) tissue paper, (3) manila paper, (4) white drawing paper, (5) construction paper, (6) tagboard, (7) flint paper, (8) foil paper, (9) gift-wrap paper, (10) cellophane paper, (11) newsprint, (12) wallpaper and (13) cardboard.

Illus. 98. Overlapping two edges of a circle's narrow slit (using either tape or glue) produces a shallow cone.

Illus. 99. The central vein of a leaf is being indented with the point of a scissors. The leaf on the right has been folded along the indented line.

of fastening you choose. For instance, tissue paper might eventually tear if stapled, whereas heavy cardboard might crack if not folded with great care. You will learn many of the special qualities of papers if you experiment in this way.

Another very useful shape is the cone. This form can be the basis for hats, baskets, figures and a number of other objects. With a pencil and compass, make a circle on a piece of paper. If you do not have a compass handy, simply outline a saucer or other round object. Cut out the circular shape and then, just as though you were slicing a piece of pie, cut out a wedge, making sure your two slits go exactly to the middle, as in Illus. 98. Join the two edges of the remaining pie together and fasten. A shallow, wide cone would require a very narrow wedge, whereas a tall, thin cone might need as much as half of the whole pie cut out. The cone at the right in Illus. 98 was formed by removing a very large wedge.

SCORING AND FOLDING PAPER

Illus. 99 illustrates the process known as scoring, that is, making a light incision, or indentation, along which you will be able to fold more easily. This is especially valuable when you are making curved folds.

Using the point of a scissors, knife, letter opener or other sharp instrument, press a line gently on to the surface of the paper. You will then be able to make a fold such as shown in the leaf in Illus. 99. You may not have to use a cutting edge—often a blunt, but fine, edge such as the non-sharp end of a nail file will do to press in a line.

MAKING A CAT-STAIRS

The cat-stairs (Illus. 101) provides an excellent source for arms, legs and long necks and tails (see

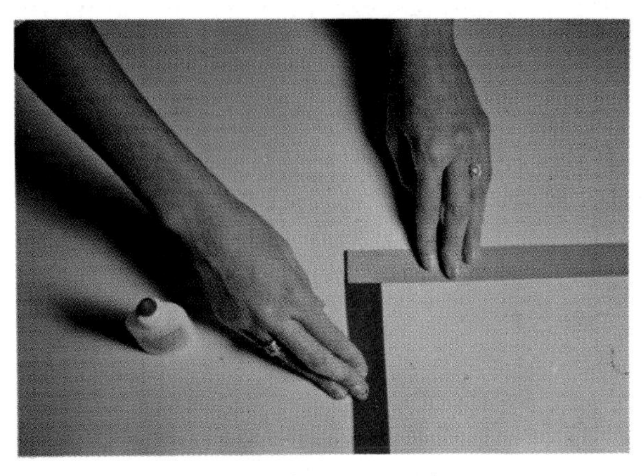

Illus. 100. Step 1 in making cat-stairs.

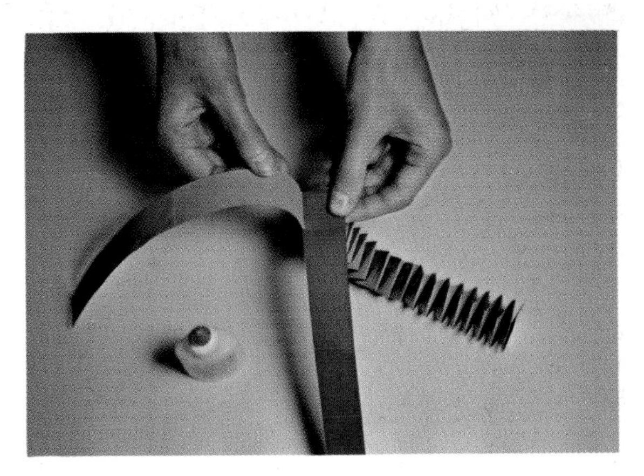

Illus. 101. Folding the cat-stairs.

Illus. 145 on page 81). Take two long strips of paper and place them together as shown in Illus. 100. Glue or staple these overlapping ends. If you use glue, wait till they are completely dry, and then fold one over the other (Illus. 101) until you reach the end. After the folding process, the strips are greatly reduced in size, so experiment first to determine the length of the strips needed to produce a cat-stairs for whatever you are making. A giraffe neck would need very long strips. If you cannot find paper large enough, you can paste extra strips on the end of your cat-stairs.

PAPER CURLING

Curled paper forms the skirt in Illus. 145 on page 81. If you want narrow curls, run the strips over the blade of a metal-edged ruler or scissors as shown in Illus. 102. Wide sheets of paper can be wound round a pencil or any other circular object of suitable size.

THREE-DIMENSIONAL PATTERNS

Incisions made into the surface of a paper object can create three-dimensional effects that suggest patterns. For instance, V-shaped slits, when the V is pulled out, simulate fish scales. Cutting and folding procedures for making three-dimensional apertures are outlined in Chapter 15.

SCRAP MATERIALS

All kinds of odd bits of scrap material can be glued, pasted, stapled, joined and twisted on to three-dimensional paper forms.

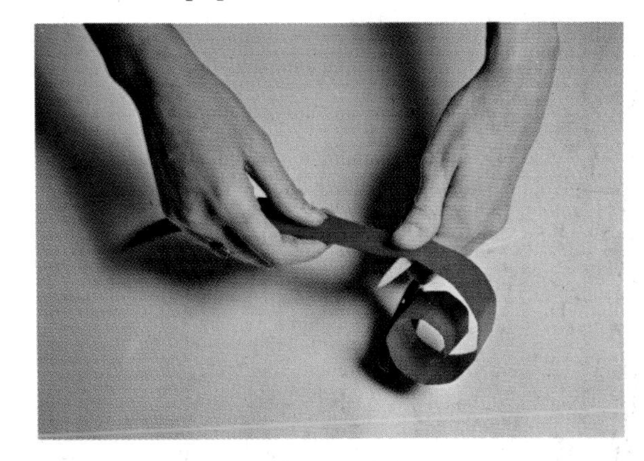

Illus. 102. Narrow strips of paper curl easily when run over a ruler or scissors.

Keep a generous supply of such things as straws, paper cups, ribbon, twine or string, wire, boxes, cloth, corks, ice cream sticks, lace, lollipop sticks, mailing tubes, matchsticks, egg and milk cartons, flash bulbs, paper doilies, pie plates, pipe cleaners, spools, tongue depressors, toothpicks, wood chips—even dried corn husks!

Use your imagination in gathering scrap—try to visualize what use you might put steel wool to, for example, or an old toothbrush or nailbrush.

Illus. 103. The children choose scrap materials to decorate their three-dimensional forms.

DECORATING WITH PAINT

There will be many times when you want to use paints on your paper sculptured objects and you should know some of their fundamental characteristics and special properties. It will aid you greatly in making your projects as attractive as possible.

When purchasing your paints, you need only acquire five colors—yellow, blue, red, black and white, since any desired hue can be achieved by mixing these basic colors. Yellow, blue and red are referred to as the *primary* colors. Whenever two primary colors are mixed together, a *secondary* color is the result. The primaries yellow and red produce the secondary color orange. Blue and red produce purple, and yellow and blue make green. You can then create six colors—three primaries and three secondaries.

However, by mixing a primary with a secondary color you can create a *tertiary* color. These consist of yellow-orange, red-orange, red-violet, yellow-green, blue-green and blue-violet.

Remember that when you mix a primary and a secondary you are actually mixing all three primaries. The result depends upon the *degree* of color that you use. For example, try mixing all three primaries

Illus. 104. A collection of joining materials; (1) brass paper fasteners, (2) common pins, (3) paper clips, (4) rubber bands, (5) masking tape, (6) rubber cement, (7) Elmer's glue, (8) white library paste, (9) Scotch tape and (10) a stapler.

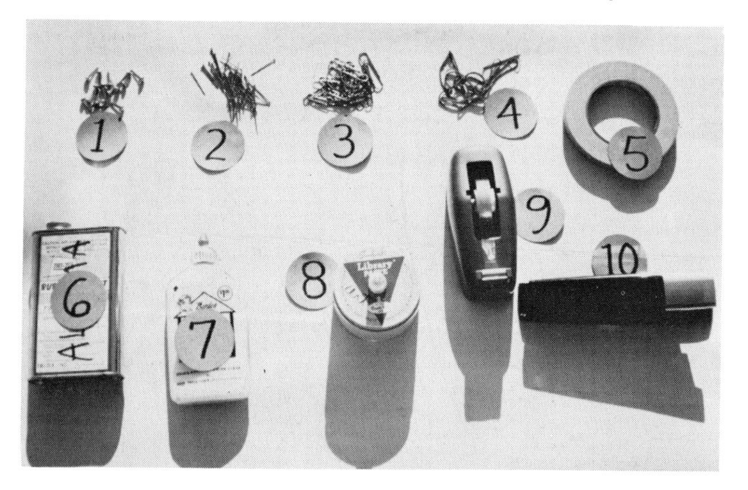

in equal amounts and see what you produce. Then mix two primaries to get a secondary which you will then mix with the remaining primary. Keep practicing until you are familiar with the results of such mixtures.

You can change the intensity of a hue, that is, make a dull color rather than a bright color. When adjacent colors on the color wheel (see Illus. 105) are mixed, the resulting color is intense or brilliant. When colors farther away from each other on the color wheel are mixed, the resulting hue is lower in intensity. Orange and green produce a dull grey color as do violet and green, and red and green. Colors opposite one another on the color wheel also produce a grey tone when mixed in equivalent proportions. Red-orange and blue-green, being opposite one another, produce a grey tone when mixed, as do yellow and purple.

Up till now you have not discovered what your black and white paints can do for you. Black will, of course, darken a hue and white will lighten it. When black is added you are creating a *shade*. When white is added you are making a *tint*. By adding both white and black you achieve a *tone*. While a tone might not be intense in color, it will have a rich appearance. Experiment with all your basic colors by first creating a shade, then a tint and then a tone.

When mixing two colors it is always advisable to begin with the lighter of the two. For instance, yellow should always be placed in the mixing pan first when the secondary color green is being made. Blue, being darker in value, is stronger than yellow, and a lesser amount is required to make green. If you put down the blue first you would have to use an enormous quantity of yellow to produce a satisfactory green.

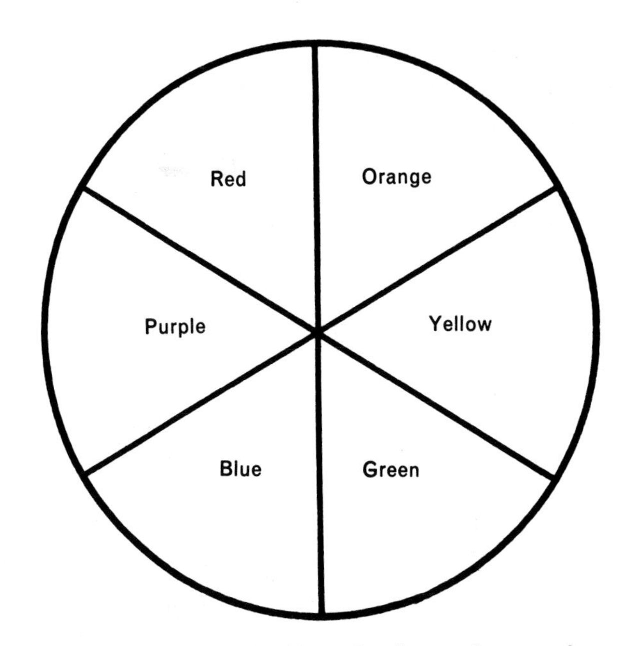

Illus. 105. The chart shows the three primary colors —red, yellow and blue, with the three secondary colors—orange, green and purple in between.

Study the primary and secondary colors in Illus. 106. You will find that a No. 5 or No. 6 bamboo brush, sometimes called a Japanese or Oriental brush (Illus. 107), is a very good brush to work with—its hairs terminate in a point, allowing you to apply thin lines, dots and shapes, as well as thick wide patterns. If a bamboo brush is not available, you may need two brushes—a thin one and a thick one.

Experiment with your brush and paints so as to achieve a variety of effects. Vary the water content to change the density of your paints. A lot of water and a limited amount of paint will enable you to create a transparent color. On the other hand, the

Illus. 106. The three squares of primary colors overlap to show the secondary colors they produce when mixed. Black is the result of mixing equal quantities of the three primary colors. (Chart from "Color In Oil Painting" by Maria and Louis DiValentin.)

dry brush technique, which you will use to paint rough, textural areas over rough paper, is simply dipping the brush into thick paint, to which little or no water is added. The dry brush is ideally suited to painting tree trunks, brick effects, or objects which have hard, opaque colors and hard, sharp edges.

You can soak your paper in clear water before adding paint to its surface. When paint is brushed on to the surface of water-soaked manila paper, a soft bleeding results. This is a good technique for painting clouds and sky. Tilt the wet paper on an angle just after you have streaked the color on in various areas so that the paint bleeds downwards, leaving some spots untouched. Try black paint for a stormy sky, orange for a sunset, and perhaps pale yellow for sunrise.

There are a number of tools and methods for adding patterns and textures to the surfaces of your paper products. Using the tip of a brush you can

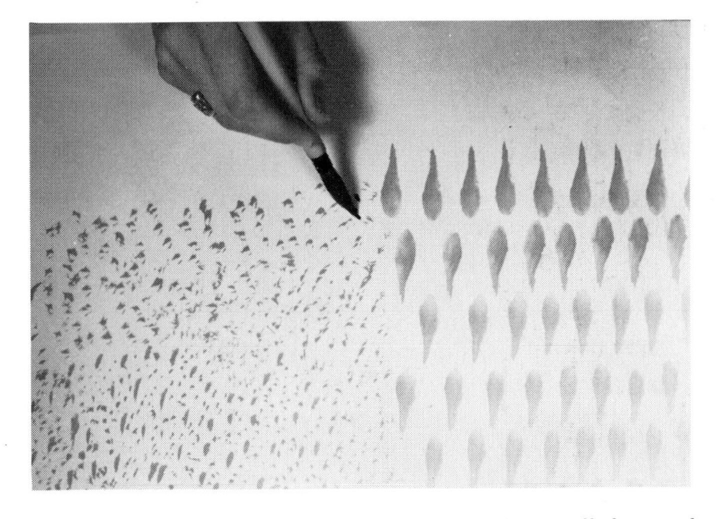

Illus. 107. Use the point of your brush to paint small dots and lines. Press the side of your brush against the paper or roll it over the paper's surface to create fat shapes and lines.

Illus. 108. A variety of designs can be created by using a wet or dry sponge on either wet or dry paper.

achieve a stippled effect, or you can roll the brush repeatedly across a surface in ½-inch intervals. Try making a variety of fat circles and blobs, tiny dots, thick lines, thin lines, triangles, squares, criss-crossed lines. Notice some of these effects in Illus. 107.

Illus. 108 shows another technique—using a sponge, either synthetic or natural, to add a textural repeat pattern to a surface. Use a dry sponge, dipped in paint, or a water-soaked sponge, dipped in paint on dry paper. Then try a paint-laden sponge, either dry or wet, on the surface of a water-soaked paper and allow the paper to dry before working with it. A crushed sheet of paper towelling or newspaper can be dipped in the same way as the sponge into paint to apply a textural repeat pattern.

The edge of a corrugated sheet of cardboard can also be used to provide a surface pattern on a paper object. Take a long, narrow piece of cardboard and fold it up as though you were making the neck of a jack-in-the-box. Using a brayer (hand roller), roll the paint on to a flat cookie sheet or a sheet of glass or tinfoil. Dip one entire long zigzag edge into the paint. Press the paint-coated edge on to the surface of whatever you are decorating. Raise it, and dip again into the paint. Continue the process until you have the desired pattern.

Another interesting means of decorating is with painted tissue paper. Crush a piece of white tissue very lightly in your hand. Unfold the paper and paste it over the surface of the paper object—using white library paste as the adhesive. Paint the desired color over the crushed tissue with very light strokes. The raised areas alone should receive the paint and the creases will remain white as in Illus. 109. Or you might work your color into all recessed and raised areas, and when dry, lightly apply a con-

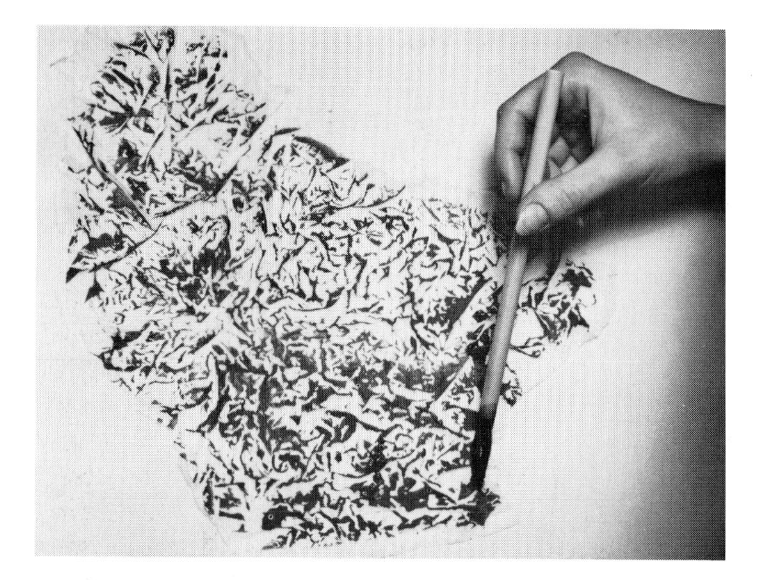

Illus. 109. Lightly painting over crinkled tissue produces a lovely stippled effect.

trasting color over the painted surface so that it only touches the raised areas.

A variety of odds and ends can be used to apply paint patterns to paper sculptures—spool ends, pieces of wood, the end of a clothespin, a thimble. Also you can "blockprint" a design from paint-dipped linoleum and wood blocks. This would of course have to be done before you do your cutting or folding.

KINDS OF PAINTS

There are two kinds of watercolor paints—one opaque and the other transparent. The opaque type is known as tempera.

Tempera paint is the most common and least expensive of all painting media. It is available in liquid form, as a powder and in cakes. When adding water to powdered tempera, mix your paint to the consistency of light cream so that it is easily controlled. It should not be so thin that it streaks. To mix, place the powdered tempera in a clean jar and add the water bit by bit until you have the right consistency. Do not add the powder to the water or you will end up with far too much paint.

Transparent watercolors are available in separate tubes and in pans, housed within a single box. The pans are less expensive and perfectly suitable for decorating paper-sculptured objects. Since these watercolors are transparent, it is sometimes difficult to cover mistakes, that is, the second color or coat will also be transparent and will not cover as well as will the opaque tempera.

Casein paint comes in both tubes and jars. By varying the quantity of water used, you can make caseins either transparent or opaque.

The most recent additions to the paint family are the new acrylics. A plastic, acrylic polymer, is mixed with pigments to form this paint. Acrylics are applied with water and will adhere to any type of paper. Colors can be painted on in transparent washes or as thick, opaque impastos. They have a great advantage in becoming waterproof when dry, as well as not cracking when the paper is bent or curled.

CRAYONS

Crayons have great potential in decoration of paper sculpture. They have three usable surfaces—

the point, the blunt end and the long side when peeled.

The point can be used to make dots and lines. The peeled side can be used to blend colors where they meet if you don't want hard lines between. Large sweeps of sky, grass, etc., can also be made quickly and easily with the long side. In addition, if you hold the peeled side of a crayon in the exact middle and sweep the ends back and forth, you will find you have a large bowlike effect. These can be overlapped. You can also twirl the crayon around in a complete circle and make a whirlpool of color. Try overlapping whirlpools of different colors. Many of the effects you achieve will suggest what use they can best be put to.

With the blunt end of the crayon, press down hard on your paper and twist. Repeat until you have a fairly constant pattern. Next, break off a small piece near the blunt end and make a repeat pattern in the same way with the jagged edge. Try holding the crayon at a 45° angle and rock the blunt end back and forth, at the same time moving up the paper. All patterns of this kind require pressure; therefore, it is essential that you make them *before* you start your three-dimensional form.

Remember that the kind of paper you are going to use will affect the texture of your crayon patterns—newsprint with its smooth surface will take on a smooth texture, construction paper a rough texture, etc.

CRAYON-RELIEF DESIGNS

The crayon-relief technique is an excellent means of producing patterns on paper objects. A full description and examples of using crayon-relief can be found on page 34.

CRAYON-STENCILED DESIGNS

Crayon stencils are very simple to make. Make or trace the star pattern in Illus. 110 A on a piece of paper with heavy crayon. Place the paper with the star in Illus. 110 face down on to the paper you will be using in your project. With an eraser, rub the outline of the star, using a heavy pressure. When you lift it up, you should have a duplicate star. Another method is to cut out the star, outline its edges in heavy crayon and again, using an eraser, smear the crayon outline on to the paper. If you do cut out the star, you can use the star-shaped hole as a second stencil (Illus. 110B). Lay it on your paper, outline again with heavy crayon and smear the crayon inwards, towards the hole. You will end up with a star that is composed of small streaks radiating towards the middle, whereas your other star will have streaks radiating outward.

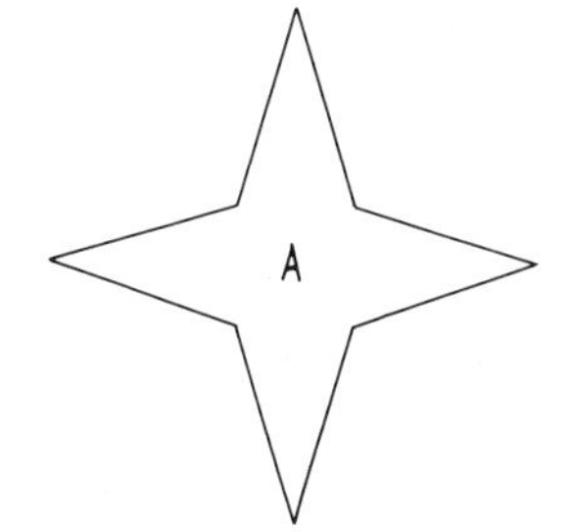

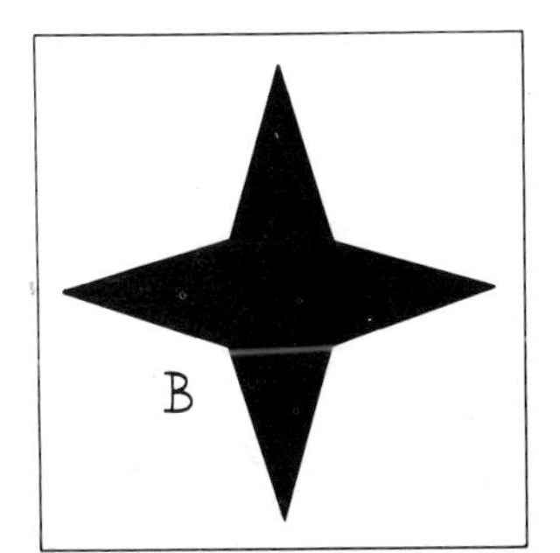

Illus. 110.

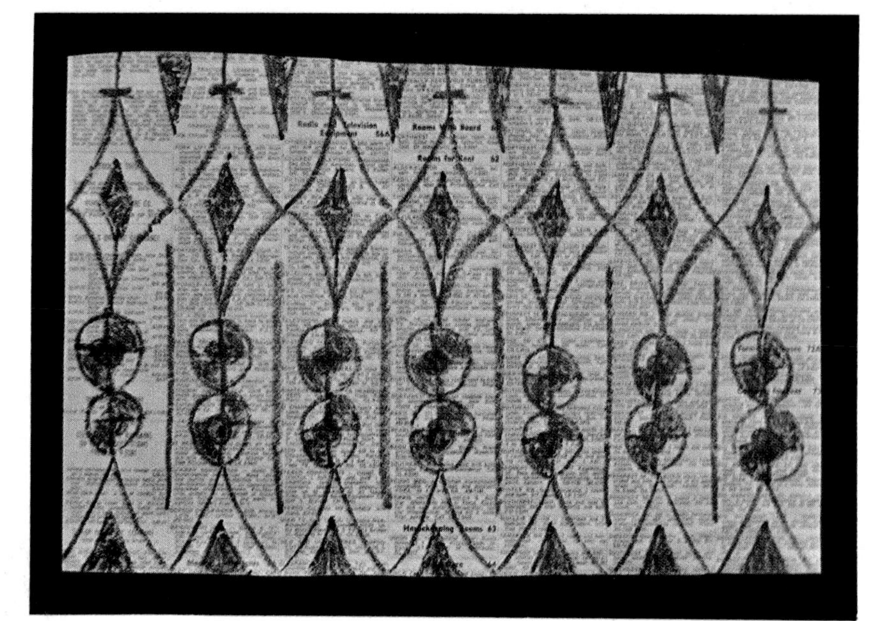

Illus. 111. Violet circles and diamonds are repeated down and across classified-ad columns, as the newspaper print offers a busy background to the design. This newspaper sheet was pasted against a piece of black construction paper, to give it greater thickness for three-dimensional forms.

CLASSIFIED AD DESIGNS

The geometric nature of news columns, particularly the classified ads, provides a strong basis for making designs with crayon. Use the horizontal and vertical lines to aid you in making the kind of design shown in Illus. 111.

THE CRAYON-ENCAUSTIC TECHNIQUE

In painting, encaustics are waxes that have been combined with colors and heated in order to fuse the color. Melted crayons can be used to color your three-dimensional projects, by applying them with stiff bristle brushes, a palette knife, tongue depressor or ice cream stick. Depending upon the temperature of the wax it will be either runny or thick and impasto-like.

There are several methods for heating crayons. If you want nothing more than a few drips of wax, simply hold the crayon over a candle. However, if you want to heat several colors at once and keep them warm and flowing, place peeled crayons in an old muffin tin, one color to a compartment. Then place the muffin tin in a large cake tin that has about 1 inch of water in it. Heat up on the stove. The hot water will keep the crayons from cooling and hardening. Small juice cans will fit nicely into a large pie plate and kept warm in the same way. Make absolutely certain that you keep the colors separate—when heated and mixed, crayons will turn grey. Tagboard provides a good surface to apply melted wax on because it is stiff and non-absorbent.

CRAYON-RESIST TECHNIQUE

A wash of tempera or other watercolor can be laid over a crayon base, which will resist the wash and produce a striking effect. A black wash is particularly effective over pastel or white crayons. However, a light wash over dark crayons results in a brilliant rich finish.

When applying crayon for the resist technique, you will have to use quite a bit of pressure. Make sure the waxy layer completely covers the paper beneath it. Work on a hard surface, using a flat sheet of paper—you cannot sculpture your paper design until after the wash has dried.

Illus. 112 is an example of what you can do with crayon-resist.

When combined with the encaustic technique, the resist method produces a glowing surface on the thick crusty areas of melted wax.

There are other resisting materials you can use instead of crayon—liquid rubber cement or floor wax. Brush them on your paper base, let dry thoroughly and then apply a wash just as before.

CRAYON-ETCHED DESIGNS

An especially interesting way of decorating many three-dimensional paper objects, such as wastebaskets, is by making an etched design. This technique may be applied after you have completed your project.

Color the entire surface of your paper object with a very heavy layer of crayon. The paper surface must, however, be a hard one, such as tagboard. Etching is particularly effective if the colors are varied and rich. Make certain the underlying paper is completely covered. Next, paint a layer of black India ink over the entire object. Allow to dry thoroughly. India ink tends to resist the wax; therefore, a good idea is to pat chalk dust or talcum powder over the crayoning first.

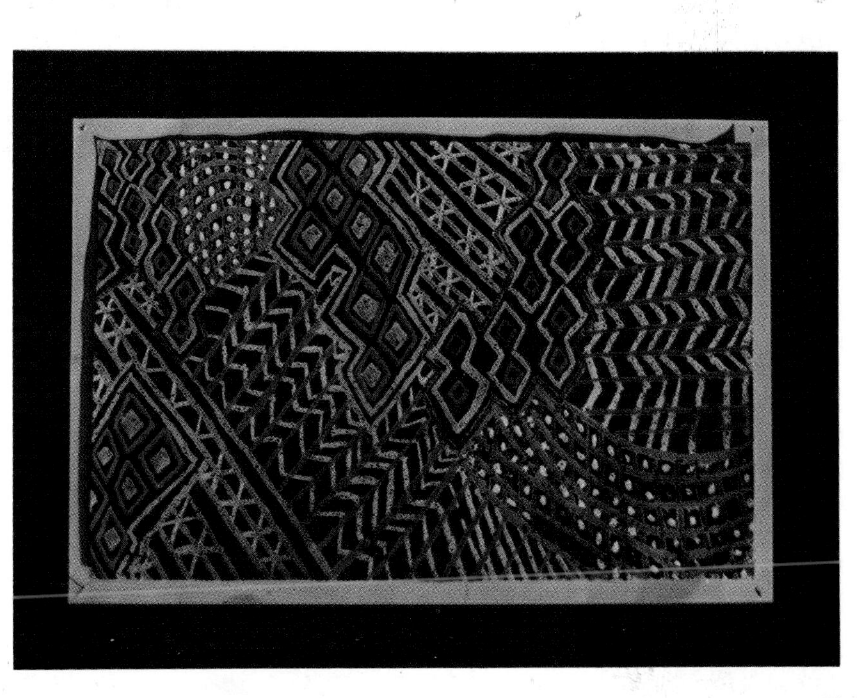

Illus. 112. An interesting crayon design on a sheet of lavender has been washed over with black watercolor. Notice how each pattern is repeated in another size, direction or shape.

Illus. 113. The varied crayon surface beneath the India ink gives the effect of colored lights touching upon the geometric design.

You are now ready to etch your design. A variety of tools can be used, all of which produce different effects. Do not limit yourself to one tool when decorating an object. A small section of a hair comb will produce wavy, evenly spaced lines. A penknife is fine for removing large areas and a tapestry or knitting needle can be used to create a delicate, controlled line. Try working with a pencil point or a nailfile.

You are now ready to start your scratching and scraping of the India ink surface. Illus. 113 shows a finished etched wastebasket, which is interesting because it displays a very well-planned etching on a crayon surface, the colors of which were obviously applied at random.

This wastebasket was constructed by placing a tagboard surface upon a gallon-sized cardboard milk carton. Crayons and ink wash were applied on a long sheet of tagboard which was then wrapped around and glued to the carton. The design was then etched with a fine pencil point. You might prefer to make your etched design before placing it on the carton, and you can make either a free or geometric design.

On the other hand, if you should want to make a very carefully planned etching, in which the colors are placed purposely so that they will show in certain places, here is what to do.

After you have decided exactly what the finished product will be, color the definite shapes and outlines that you want. On a large sheet of tracing paper, draw around these color areas, and label them according to their colors. In this way, after you have covered the crayon surface with the ink wash, you can use this sheet of paper as a guide to the colors underneath. Then you can correlate your etched lines accordingly.

Other materials can be substituted for India ink. Heavy black crayon or a wash of black tempera mixed with powdered or liquid detergent serve well as etching surfaces. Be sure to use chalk dust or powder before applying the tempera. However, if you want to crayon-etch small areas and plan on using a tempera wash, dip the brush into the black tempera and then brush lightly on a bar of soap or a piece of raw potato and mix slightly. Then apply the mixture to the crayoned surface.

Do not worry if you make a mistake in your etching. You can easily rectify it by placing more India ink, tempera or black crayon over the etched lines and then re-etching.

Crayon-etched designs are very easily damaged. The blackened surface might get accidentally scratched or broken. To avoid this, paint your finished paper product with a coat of shellac or light varnish.

CHALK DESIGNS

Colored chalk is one of the easiest and most economical mediums for paper-sculpture decoration. Although it is somewhat limited in that it can only be used on dull-surfaced papers (it flakes off shiny paper), you will find many opportunities to use it.

Chalk comes in many colors and is available in two varieties—soft chalk which is made from alabaster and is quite inexpensive, and dustless chalk which is somewhat harder and has the added advantage of being nonallergenic.

Facial tissue or cloth can be used to soften and blend chalks. A commercial fixative or hair spray can be sprayed on to chalk designs to avoid their being rubbed off.

Chalk-stenciled designs can be applied in the same way as you did with crayons and are particularly effective when a colored chalk is smeared on to a paper of a contrasting color.

White powdered tempera paint and colored chalk can be mixed so that the paint acts as a fixative. Soak your paper in water and shake about one teaspoon of powdered paint on the surface. With a brush, blend the water and powder together, spreading it until the entire surface is coated with white paint. While the paint is still quite damp, apply your color designs, using the side of the chalk. When dry, the color will not rub off.

There are two other fixatives you might experiment with—sugar and buttermilk. You can add sugar to water-soaked paper in the same way as the powdered paint and it will hold the chalk very nicely. Or "paint" your paper with buttermilk before applying the chalk design. All of these processes must of course be done before you cut and sculpture your three-dimensional object.

Illus. 114. Three-dimensional people are fun to make.

Illus. 115. Monofold animals provide excellent physical characteristics that lend themselves to paper decoration—such as this lion's wood-shaving mane and tail.

6. Monofold Figures

Because of their body symmetry, both animals and people are ideally suited as subjects for the making of three-dimensional, single-folded forms. However, our animals will be constructed on a horizontal fold and our people on a vertical fold, that is, the animal shapes will be mirror images from side to side, and the people shapes from front to back. (See Illus. 114 and 115.)

MONOFOLD ANIMALS

While the lion shown in Illus. 115 is constructed from three different pieces of folded paper, one each for the head, body and tail, we will start by making an animal from two pieces of paper. Take a large sheet of construction paper and fold in two in the direction shown in Illus. 116. Using a felt-tip pen, outline the body of your animal and cut it out with the paper still folded as shown in Illus. 117. Since our animal is a llama, it has a nice straight back that corresponds to the folded edge.

Next, cut a 2-inch slit, starting from the right edge, along the fold. This slit will serve to accommodate the long neck and head piece. Now, in the same way, draw and cut out the neck and head. Place the neck in the slit and glue it between the two layers, pressing together until dry (Illus. 118).

Illus. 119 shows the finished llama. Notice that his legs are fatter than a real llama's would be—this is done to provide a good support. A synthetic

Illus. 116.

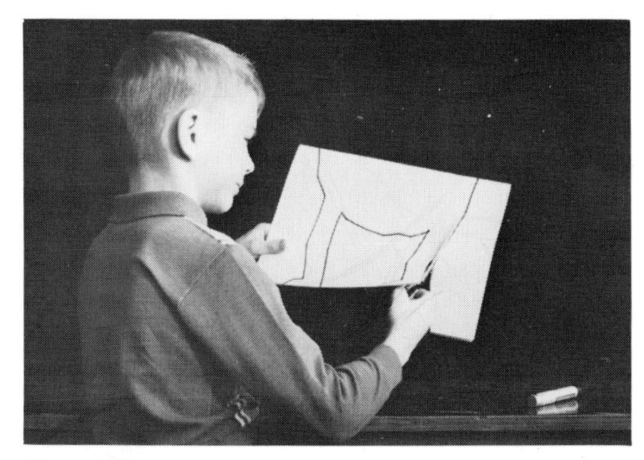

Illus. 117.

Illus. 118.

Illus. 119. Just one fold transforms a flat, two-dimensional sheet of paper into a three-dimensional standing form.

Illus. 120. Although this donkey is made of two pieces, he might have been made from a single piece of paper, since his head falls lower than his back. The two baskets are formed of rectangular sheets shaped into cylinders and draped over the animal's back with narrow strips of paper. A tinfoil star decorates the rectangular construction-paper pads, and a piece of paper cut on the diagonal into slits makes a realistic tail.

sponge, dipped into tempera paint, produced the interesting pattern on the llama's sides. The ear and eye were both cut from construction paper. Fringed paper forms the eyelashes.

The camel in Illus. 121 was made from a single piece of construction paper, with the exception of the head. When an animal's head naturally falls lower than the back, which of course is formed by the fold, you can use a single piece. Here, for example, the neck was cut out from the same piece as the body, since it is on a level with the body. The head was then pasted on to the neck.

Notice that because the animal's legs are slender, support is provided by pipe cleaners glued to the inner sides.

The two canteens are formed of cubes and are held by a chain constructed of paper strips draped over one hump. By glueing the ends of one strip together to make a circle, then threading the next

Illus. 121.

strip through the circle and glueing that one together, and so on, you will end up with several chainlike links. Narrow strips of black paper form the halter.

Illus. 122 shows a turtle with a two-piece construction. The unusual design is composed of very narrow strips of newspaper which were curled up tightly and pasted on the sides. This effect could also suggest the wool of a sheep or the curly hair of a poodle.

Illus. 122.

Our camel in Illus. 123 is made out of one piece of paper. The fold follows the line between the two humps and the top of the head. The decorative pattern on the camel's side was formed by cutting a number of small slits so that tabs could be pulled forward. The tabs were then curled slightly. (See Chapter 15 for instructions on making other three-dimensional protrusions.)

Cotton batting makes a soft furry coat for the cat shown in Illus. 124. The batting has been pulled apart and flattened out to make a thin layer which was then pasted on to the cat's side. This cat was made out of three pieces of paper, one each for the

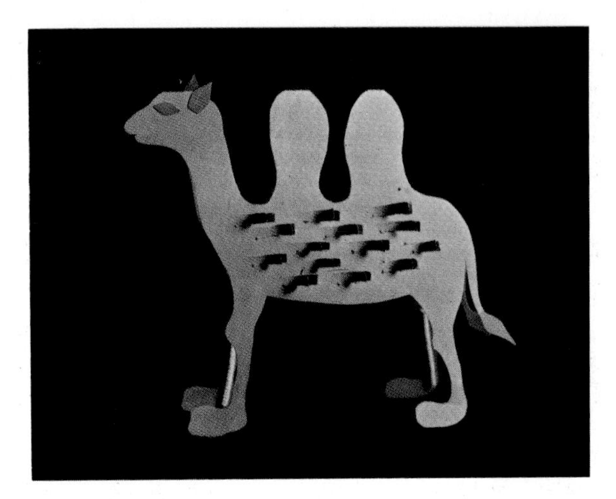
Illus. 123.

head, body and tail. Decorative touches include pipe-cleaner whiskers, button eyes and a shiny red ribbon. Try to think of how you might simulate the characteristics of a striped tabby cat, or a Siamese, or one of the big cats, such as a panther or tiger. Most animals have distinctive markings or features that make them ideal subjects for decorated monofold projects.

Illus. 124.
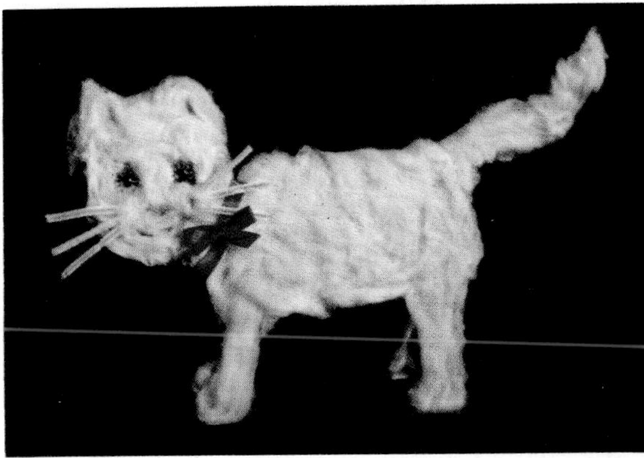

Illus. 125. Here is a single-fold construction that was done somewhat differently from our other animals. The fold was made on the diagonal, rather than on the horizontal, and the giraffe outline was drawn on the triangular shape that resulted. The original fold runs along the highest part of the back to the head.

MONOFOLD PEOPLE

Three-dimensional paper people offer an opportunity to exercise a great deal of imagination. Here, in addition to portraying people from various professions, occupations, stories, or from history, you can add a very important touch—character. Although most of your characterizations will be in the form of decorative techniques, remember that the way people stand or hold their heads and their bodies very often is a key to their character or personality.

The man and woman in Illus. 126 are both made up of two main parts. From the waist down, they are three-dimensional, that is, made up of a folded piece of paper. From the waist up, they are two-dimensional—made from a single piece of paper which was pasted to the lower section.

Hair, eyebrows, eyes and mouths are all made of pieces of colored construction paper, as well as the dress collar, belt and trimmings. The woman's yellow construction-paper hair is slitted and rolled back on the ends to make it curly. She also has slitted and curled eyelashes.

Try to imagine what kind of people they are—from their clothes, expressions, etc.

Illus. 126.

Illus. 127.

Illus. 129. A fairy princess waves a tinfoil wand. Her pale pink tissue-paper apron is gathered together and glued to her waist so that its folds form a three-dimensional effect over her monofold skirt. Crepe paper might make a ruffled skirt. Her rakish clown companion wears a tasseled cone hat and cat-stairs ruffles around his neck, wrists and ankles.

Illus. 128. This lanky sheriff is ready for action. His three-dimensional bowlegs were cut out first from a folded piece of paper (Illus. 127). Notice how suggestive they are of a cowboy. Then his two-dimensional torso and head were cut from another piece and pasted on at the waist. Bright tissue paper provides a colorful scarf, and tinfoil, ideal for his badge, guns and spurs, is also used to make a gleaming hatband. Different-colored construction papers form a hat, belt and holsters, boots and vest. A crayon-checkered shirt completes his outfit.

Illus. 130. People from foreign countries that have national costumes are easy to make. It's not difficult to guess where these two come from.

Illus. 131. A lady from Spain wears a headpiece of real bird feathers and a real bead necklace and carries a folded paper fan. Realistic pleats and ruffles on her skirt and blouse were made with crayon.

Illus. 132. A doctor and nurse are ready for an important case. Their necks and her arms are made of cat-stairs. The nurse wears a three-dimensional cap. As she takes her first step towards the operating room, her feet are kept one behind the other by a small folded paper stand.

Illus. 133. Why not make a bride and groom as place-cards for the wedding reception? This bride wears a gown of paper covered with a fine sheer cloth and white lacy ribbons and a sheer cloth veil.

Illus. 134. The circus is in town. A brave lion tamer is all decked out in a construction-paper outfit and whip. His demure bareback-rider companion wears a cone skirt and laced ballet shoes of white paper strips. Notice that her slim legs require a support.

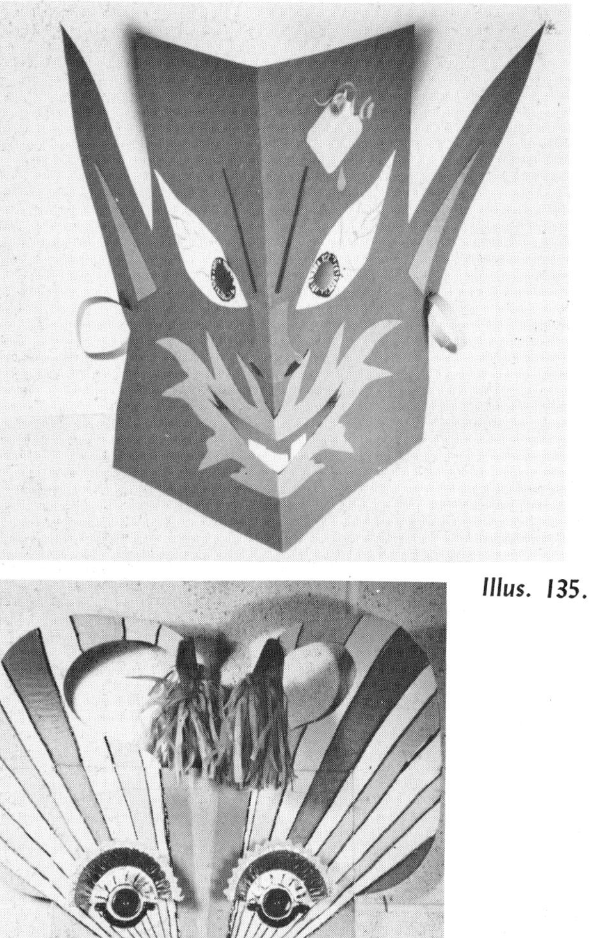

Illus. 135.

Illus. 136.

MONOFOLD MASKS

Among the many single-fold creations that are possible besides people and animals, you will certainly enjoy mask-making. Masks are simple to make and you will be following a tradition that dates back to the cavemen! Although pre-historic people used masks to ward off evil spirits, your masks might be more in the ancient Greek and Roman tradition of drama. Costume parties and Halloween festivities both call for masks, but after your first mask creation you will probably find yourself making them just for the fun of it.

We tend to think of masks as being grotesque, but you can make a happy Cinderella face, an appealing puppy, a proud Queen, or a mysterious Batman. You can really test your ingenuity by trying to make a mask to signify a certain kind of person or profession such as a doctor, a lawyer or a corporation chief!

Your masks will of course be symmetrical, so choose enough similar paper pieces to allow repeating colors and shapes on each side of the face. Crayon or paint will help greatly in defining features and in conveying mood.

Our mask in Illus. 135 is made from a single piece of construction paper. The simple cutting involved nothing more than carving out a pair of devilish ears. After that the paper was folded through the middle. As you can see, a three-dimensional mask fits the contours of the face. Two brass paper fasteners, one at the base of each ear can hold a rubber band which can be slipped over the wearer's head. Paper-strip earrings and a fire-eating construction-paper mouth add fiendish touches.

Illus. 136 is an example of the kind of mask you can make from corrugated cardboard. First out-

Illus. 137. A fierce witch-doctor mask, decorated with tinfoil and pipe cleaners and intensely colored tempera paints, is made from corrugated cardboard.

line your mask shape on a sheet of folded newspaper. Then trace it on to the cardboard. Use tempera or crayon to emphasize shapes and color. Our mask has tinfoil pot-pie eyelashes and button eyeballs.

Build up the surfaces of your monofold masks by adding noses or big chins from a papier-mâché substance, consisting of facial or bathroom tissue soaked in diluted Elmer's glue. This will make very satisfactory protruding, or three-dimensional, features—even cheekbones or eyebrows.

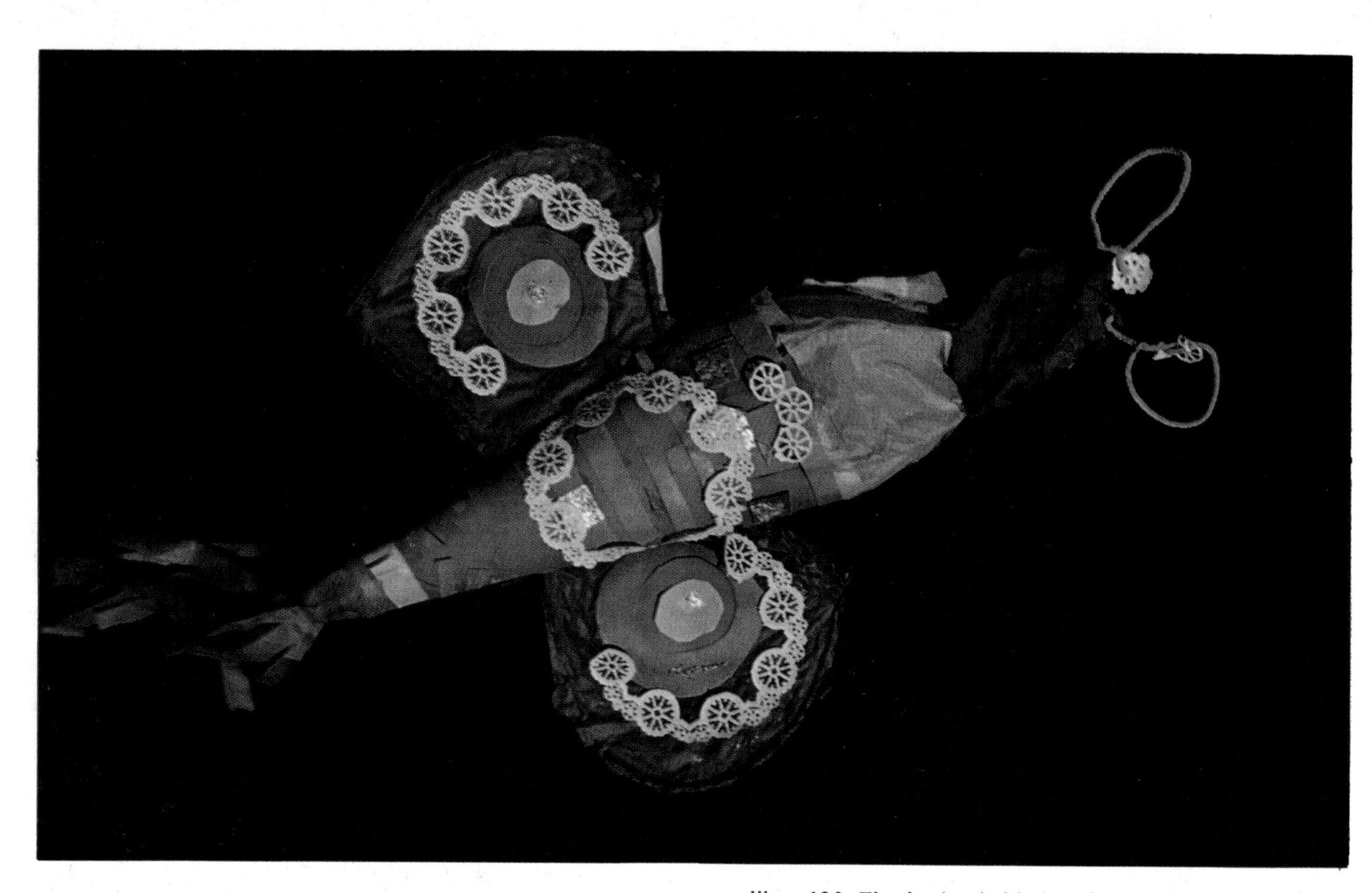

Illus. 138. The basis of this imaginative flying insect is a simple paper cone as shown in Illus. 139. Pipe cleaners make up various parts of the skeleton, such as the wings, the pale blue front section of the body, and the head. Tissue paper is glued on to these frames which are stapled to the body cone. Small shapes cut from a paper doily, and construction-paper circles add touches of color on the wings. The tail is composed of tissue-paper strips.

Illus. 139.

7. Cone Creations

CONE PEOPLE

The cone shape forms a perfect basis for creating three-dimensional people. The Spanish dancer in Illus. 143, believe it or not, is—underneath it all—a cone. The designs on her outfit were accomplished by the crayon-relief technique.

Place thin sheets of newsprint over three different-patterned and different-sized plastic doilies. Using the side of a peeled crayon, rub each doily until the patterns show through (Illus. 140). Now cut out each pattern, and cut a circle through the middle of each. The largest piece of paper should have the largest central circle, etc. (Illus. 141). Fit the circles over the cone and place tape against the top side of each circle and against the side of the cone to hold them in place. Slightly crease to make them fluff out and down (Illus. 142).

Illus. 143.

Illus. 140.

Illus. 141.

Illus. 142.

Illus. 144. This colorful Latin dancer has a skirt made of 25 tissue-paper circles placed over a cone.

The stunning Mexican dancer in Illus. 144 has a 25-tiered skirt! Each tier was cut from colored tissue paper, starting with the largest at the bottom and gradually getting smaller and smaller. After the middle of each piece was cut out proportionately, one by one they were placed over a narrow tall paper cone.

Patterned wallpaper forms her blouse and her shiny belt is made of red ribbon. Pipe-cleaner necklaces and bracelets and a three-dimensional hat complete the picture. As before, the torso was glued on to the top of the cone.

Besides tissue, crepe paper makes an ideal skirt material for a cone figure. Cut a strip slightly wider than the distance from the waist of the cone figure to the floor. Wrap the strip around the cone, making sure the grain of the paper runs in a vertical direction. Shirr the material around the waist and hold in place with a rubber band. If you put a small piece of tape on the band, it will not creep up towards the top of the cone. Using thumbs and forefingers, stretch the lower border of the skirt so that it fans out in a bell-like shape. It is also possible to use cloth in the same way.

Illus. 145 shows still another skirt-construction method. Many closely spaced horizontal strips of paper were placed round the cone. Vertical slits were then cut into the paper as in Illus. 146, and curled up and back to make the ruffly effect.

From beneath a unique construction-paper shawl emerge two springy cat-stairs arms which complement the pattern of the skirt.

A table-tennis-ball head supporting strands of glued-on binder-twine hair is topped by a three-dimensional hat. The hat is a very shallow cone. Close to the bottom edge of the cone, a circular score line was made and the edge folded back. Near

Illus. 145. Another effective skirt design. Here paper strips were wound horizontally round the cone figure. To achieve the ruffles, vertical slits are cut into each paper strip and curled up.

Illus. 146. These are the slit placements for the ruffled skirt in Illus. 145.

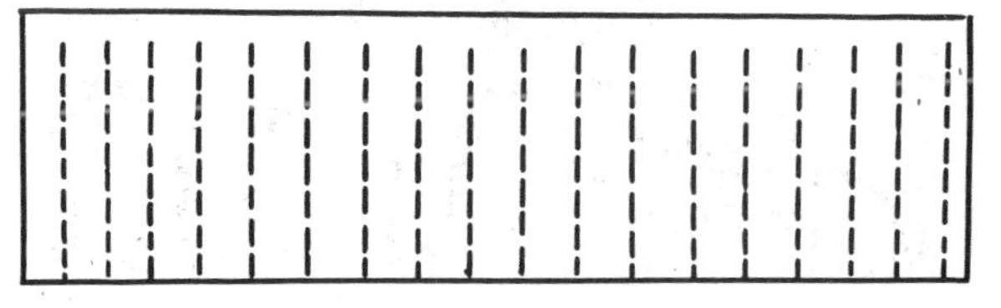

Illus. 147. To make this squared-off cone, fold it in half and then in half again so that you have four vertical creases. Plump it out so that it looks somewhat like this skirt—its appearance will vary according to the kind of cone you make. This fine lady has ruffles and hair made by cutting and curling strips of paper.

Illus. 148. Here a cone is not actually part of the figure. Instead it forms a stand against which a two-dimensional boy figure is pasted. His fancy dinner jacket has a crayon-relief pattern. You could make another figure and paste it on to the other side of the cone—perhaps the girl friend he's bringing the candy to!

Illus. 149. This little chorus is made up of a variety of papers. The angel at the left with the tinfoil halo is made of a white drawing paper cone with a Christmas-glitter border. Construction paper forms the middle chorister completely and the legs, head and hat of the singer on the right, whose torso and arms are made of wallpaper. Notice his cone-shaped legs.

the peak of the cone, another score line was made along which the paper was folded inwards, allowing a shallow depression to accommodate the ball.

The figure in Illus. 145 does not require a two-dimensional top. Here, a head can be placed directly on to the top of the cone. If you use a table-tennis ball, cut a hole in the bottom so it can be "screwed" on. Or press a dent in the ball and flatten the top of the cone and glue them together.

The jaunty drum major in Illus. 150 differs from our other cone figures. Only his torso is formed from a cone to which are attached his head, legs and arms. A table-tennis ball is used again for a head. Paper legs and arms were made separately and glued on. Notice that his legs are too weak to support him, so a little cardboard support has been pasted to his back. Cat-stairs arms provide not only a decorative touch but allow him to assume a typical baton-twirler pose. Some Christmas glitter to add sparkle, a pipe-cleaner baton, and a monofold paper hat are all that are needed and our drum major is ready to lead the band.

Illus. 150.

Illus. 151. Nothing stirs the imagination more than a creature from outer space. This surprised-looking little fellow has a furry rabbit-tail face and extraordinary antennae made of pipe cleaners and cotton batting. Unusually long cat-stairs limbs emphasize his bizarre nature. Your space creature might have propellers, strange tentacles coming from various parts of the cone, gigantic protruding eyes, or tennis-ball ears.

CONE CREATURES

The base of the owl in Illus. 153 is a very fat shallow cone. To make the head, fold a sheet of paper and cut out the head, using the fold line as the top of the skull. Then drape the folded head over the cone body and glue it to the front and back sides. The wings too can be made from a single-folded piece of paper, or else each wing separately, and joined to the body with brass fasteners. If you make them from a single sheet, attach them to the front of the cone before glueing the head on.

This owl has a three-dimensional feather pattern achieved by cutting slits and pushing them through. Make monofold ears and glue them on each side of the head. Colored pipe cleaners make

Illus. 152. This fellow obviously comes from still another planet, and judging from the sunglasses, a bright one. Bent pipe cleaners form his arms and legs, to which are attached sponge hands and feet. Strips of insulation foam make a rare head.

excellent bird legs and feet as you can see, as well as owlish spectacles.

The magnificient peacock in Illus. 154 is made from three construction-paper cones—one large body cone, a smaller neck cone and a tiny head cone (Illus. 155).

Different-colored tissue papers were cut in strips, curled over a scissors' blade and then alternate colors were attached to the body cone and neck with glue.

Pipe cleaners were stapled by their ends to the top rim of the body cone (Illus. 155) to form the basis of the tail. Then tissue paper in the same colors was cut in elongated teardrop shapes. The edges of each shape were slit and curled over the scissors' blade. Notice that the tail has three sections corresponding to the three pipe cleaners. The tail sections are decorated with contrasting peacock-like spots which were cut in teardrop and circular shapes.

The head was covered with curled green tissue

Illus. 153.

Illus. 154. Bird forms are well suited to a cone frame since generally their bodies taper at one end, as do their heads. While there are many birds you might make from a single cone, this peacock was constructed from three.

Illus. 155. This is the basic structure for the peacock in Illus. 154. The tail section is composed of three pipe cleaners stapled on to the body cone.

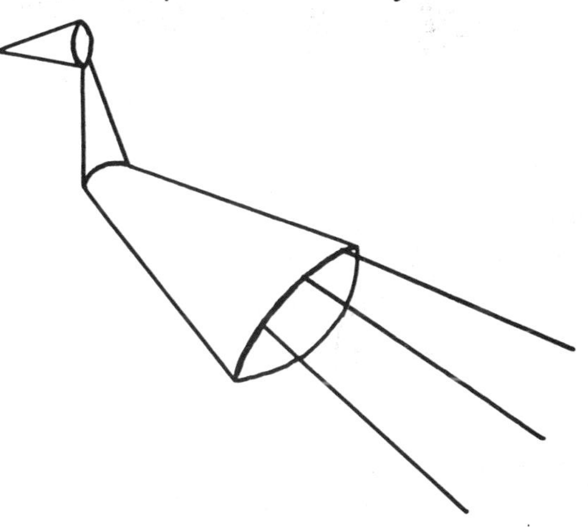

paper which, like the tail sections, was glued in place. The large construction-paper feet are fastened to pipe cleaners with staples.

The cat-stairs are wonderfully effective in forming the legs and tail of the 2-foot-high cone cat in Illus. 156. They are secured to the cone body by brass paper fasteners. Large, two-dimensional paper paws are attached to the ends of the cat-stairs and have tiny pipe-cleaner claws. A two-dimensional wallpaper head sports three-dimensional eyelashes and whiskers made of paper strips, narrowly slitted and curled, and a small paper cone nose.

Illus. 156.

Illus. 157.

The pink tissue-paper bow adds a demure look to this sly cellophane-eyed cat.

A wide paper cone forms the body for the satisfied-looking squirrel in Illus. 157. His head is composed of two separate but identical cut-outs that are pasted on either side of the cone body and touch each other only from the nose down.

His paper legs are attached at the hip joint with brass fasteners and his cat-stairs arms end in two little paper paws that are clutching a real walnut. That big bushy squirrel-tail effect is achieved by making a sturdy base of at least three layers of construction paper and pasting many narrow strips of crepe paper on to it. Cardboard would also serve as a substantial support for the upright tail. The squirrel's fine whiskers are made of broom bristles.

Illus. 158. What is this? It could be an animal never seen before—like a whang-doodle. Flat, red, webbed feet are pasted to cat-stairs legs. Naturally, this animal has two tails. The lower, short one, is made of paper strips pasted to the inside of the upper edge of the cone and curled upward. The second tail is long and frondlike and rises to much greater heights. Long, narrow colorful strips of tissue paper were glued to pipe cleaners which were stapled to the upper rim of the cone body.

Illus. 159. This fanciful mouse is made of three cones. The two rear cones are glued by their tips to the inside bottom of the cone in front. He has tiny cone eyes with bead eyeballs and pipe-cleaner eyebrows and nose. Cellophane-covered pipe cleaners are glued to his middle cone and extend as feelers or antennae.

CONE HATS

The cone is a perfect shape for making a hat. The simplest hat you could make is a very tall paper cone held together with staples and with a chin tie of string attached to either side of the base with brass fasteners.

Illus. 160 shows a simple hat. Here a large scalloped paper circle, with the middle cut out, is taped to the bottom of the cone to make a brim. Curled tissue-paper strips form a gay pompon on top and a decoration in the middle of each scallop on the brim. You might make this hat out of a bright shiny gold or red foil.

You can use many scrap materials in making cone hats—glitter, ribbon, sequins—or you might want to paint a hat with temperas. If you use such techniques as crayon resist or crayon encaustic, you should do it before sculpturing your hat.

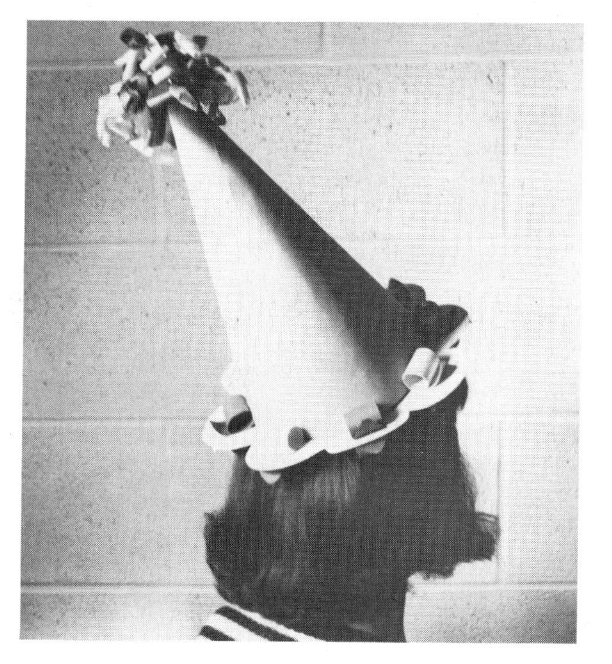

Illus. 160.

Illus. 161.

Holidays suggest many ideas for decorating hats—valentines, angels, witches or bunnies. The New Year's hat in Illus. 161 has a construction-paper cone base with tissue-paper decoration. A pinking shears makes the irregular edges on the pink and red tissue strips. Curled tissue paper strips shape a fancy tuft at the tip of the cone and uncurled strips make the bow-like tufts on the front of the hat.

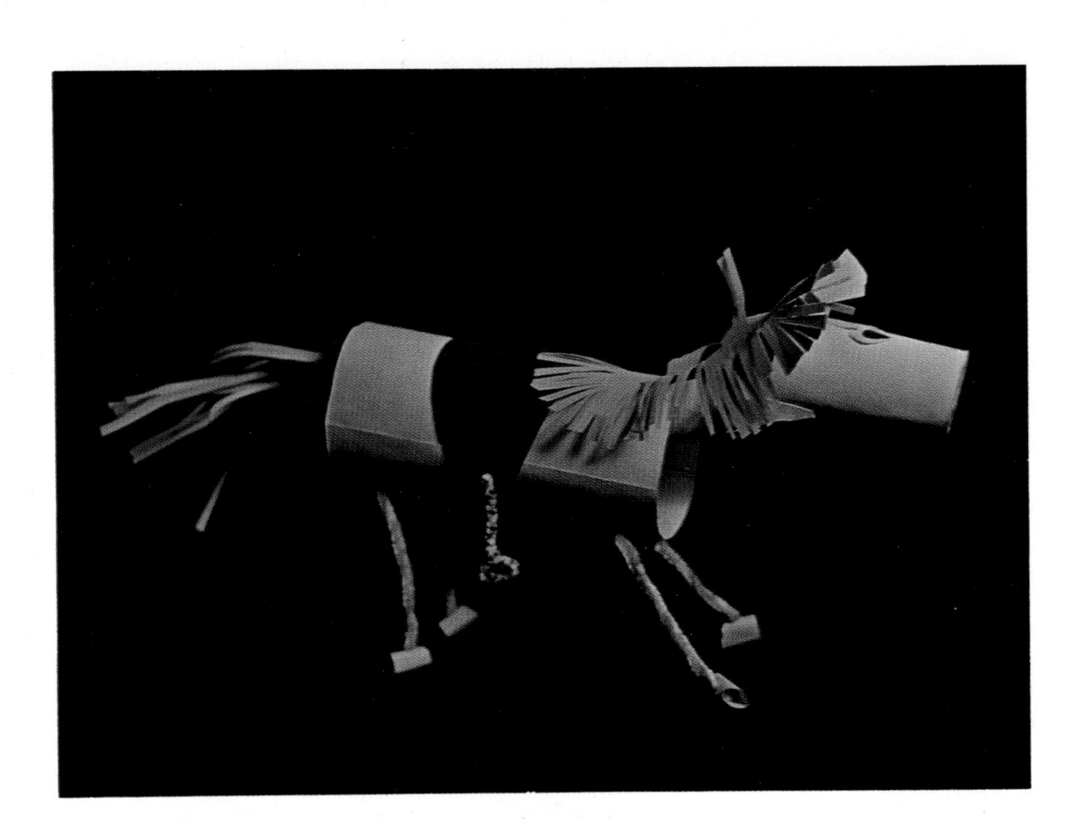

Illus. 162. Cylindrical shapes form the head, neck, body and even the hoofs of this pink and blue horse. Pipe-cleaner legs and stirrups are poked into the body, and slitted construction paper makes an effective tail and mane.

8. Cylindrical Creatures

Have you ever stopped to think of how many of nature's forms are shaped like the cylinder in Illus. 163? Tree trunks, caterpillers, animal and human legs and arms, torsos. Try to think of as many cylindrical shapes as possible before starting your cylinder projects.

Illus. 163.

CYLINDRICAL STABILES

As you remember, we made a simple woven-paper stabile in Chapter 1. By now you are ready to experiment with more complicated stabiles. To make the stabile shown in Illus. 166, fold vertically a large sheet of construction paper at various in-

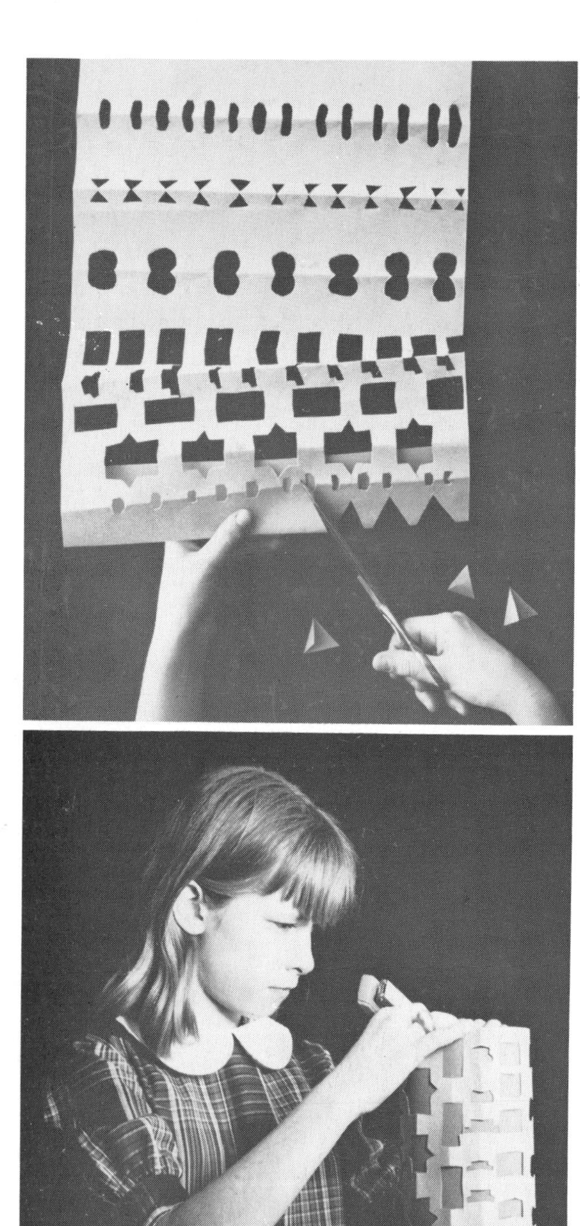

Illus. 164.

Illus. 165.

Illus. 166.

tervals, and, starting with the first fold, cut out little shapes as shown in Illus. 164. Notice each line has similar shapes, but all lines differ from one another.

The cut-out design can then be placed over a contrasting sheet of construction paper of the same size which has been shaped into a cylinder too. Staple the ends together (Illus. 165) and you have a multi-sided, geometric-patterned stabile that will brighten up a coffee table, desk, or wherever a splash of color is needed.

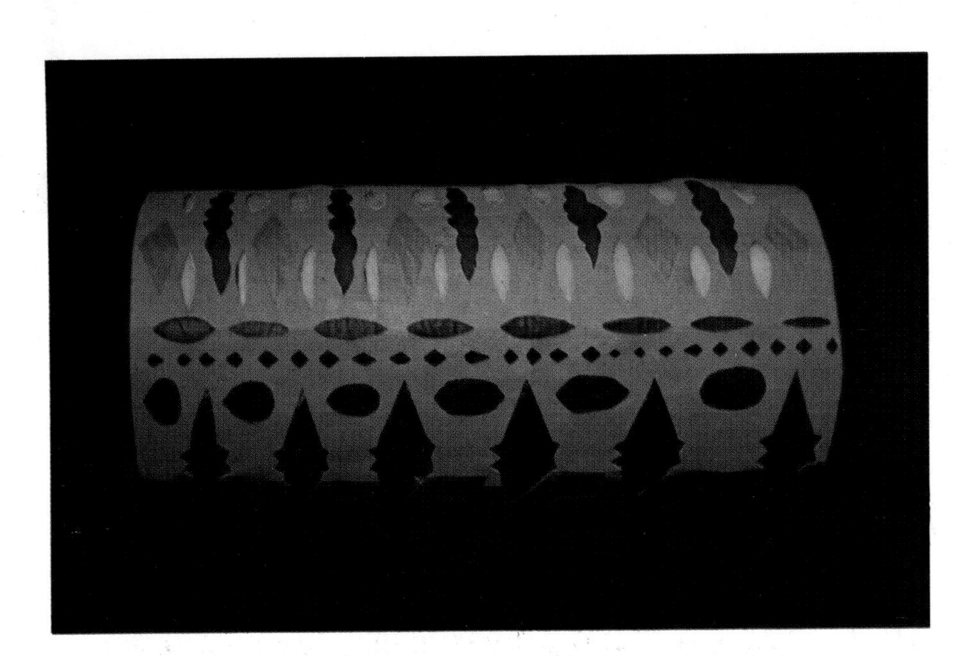

Illus. 167. Although this stabile was constructed in the same manner as that in Illus. 166, the tissue and cellophane colors showing through the little window shapes were pasted on individually along the reverse side of the orange paper before it was sculptured. The same color was used along each row.

Illus. 168. Here are four examples of variety of shape, size, and pattern you should strive for when creating stabiles.

The stabile in Illus. 169 has a cylinder at its core. To begin, cut evenly spaced parallel slits into a sheet of colored construction paper, beginning perpendicular to the paper's fold. Each slit should end about 1 inch from the ends (Illus. 170). (Does this procedure remind you of anything? It should—this is how you made your first paper loom for weaving in Chapter 1.) Then form the unfolded slitted sheet into a cylindrical shape. Make a simple cylinder from another piece of construction paper, at least 1½ inch smaller than the first and in a contrasting color. Place the slitted cylinder around the second one and staple the opposite ends of the outer sheet to the inner one (Illus. 171). The shorter the inner cylinder is, the wider the strips of the outer one will fan out. A tall inner cylinder would cause the fan to draw up somewhat.

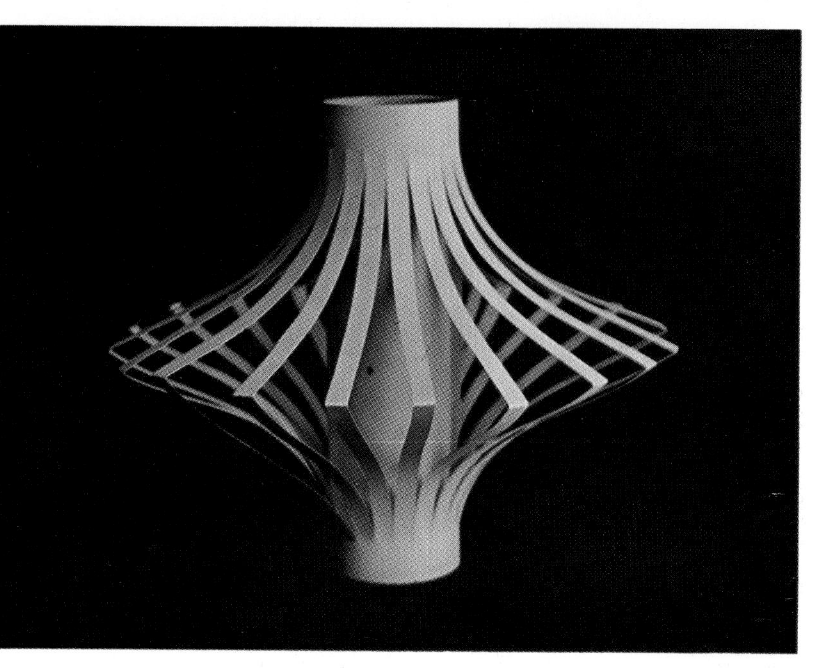

Illus. 169.

Illus. 170.

Illus. 171.

The more elaborate stabile in Illus. 172 is composed of three sections with a cardboard tube core. Each section was cut out as before, but instead of cutting into one sheet of construction paper, two sheets were folded and cut at the same time for each section, giving a two-color effect. The foundation tube was covered with colored tinfoil and cellophane, so little glints would show through the openings of the slitted radiating cylinders. Notice that the middle section fans out further than the two end pieces. Bands of orange tissue not only

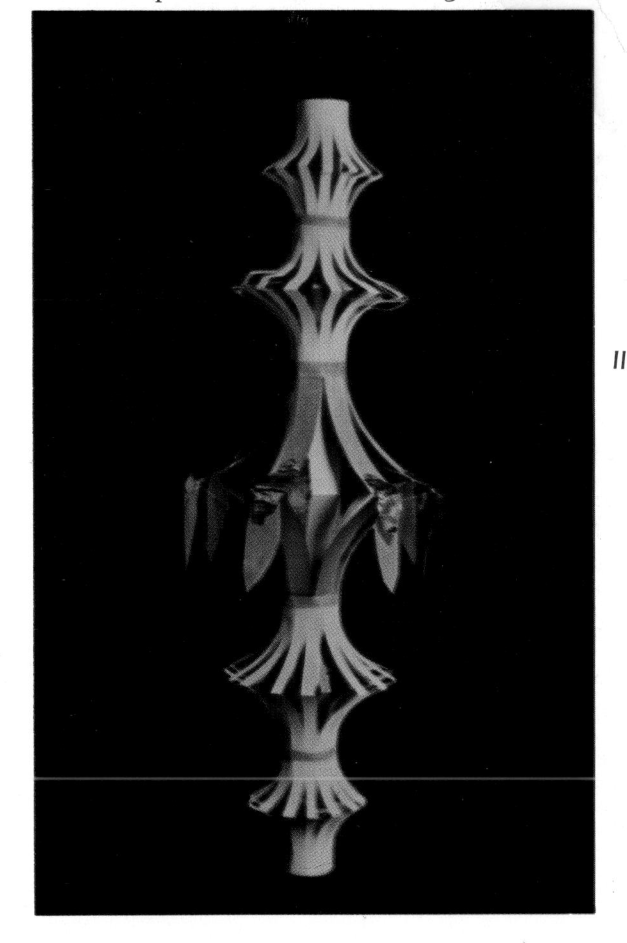

Illus. 172.

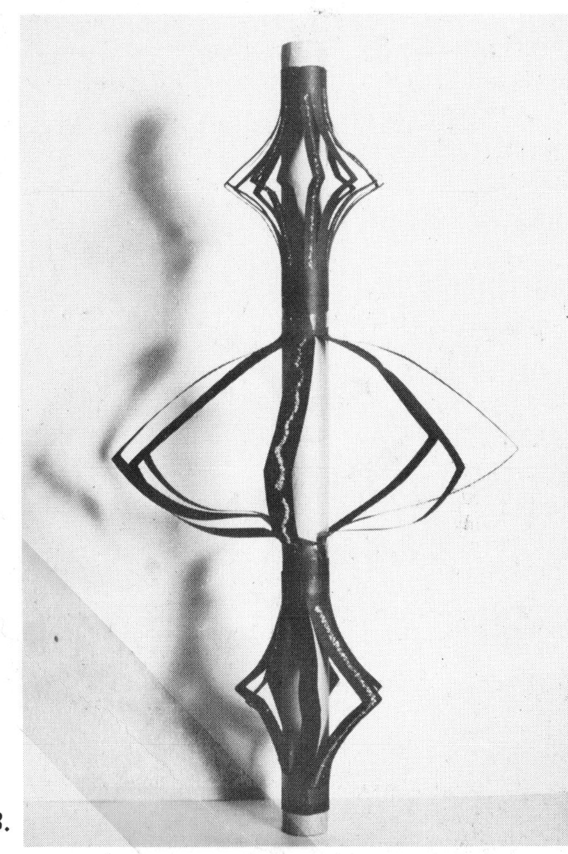

Illus. 173.

cover the joints of the sections, but add a pleasing color contrast. Orange tissue and silver tinfoil, glued to the central protrusions, provide a focal point of interest.

The lantern stabile in Illus. 173 was made in very much the same way. Three pieces of black construction paper were cut into slitted cylinders and placed around a cardboard tube which is covered with sheets of different-colored tissue paper. The central slitted paper was made longer than the two ends so that it could be squashed together enough to protrude far beyond the ends.

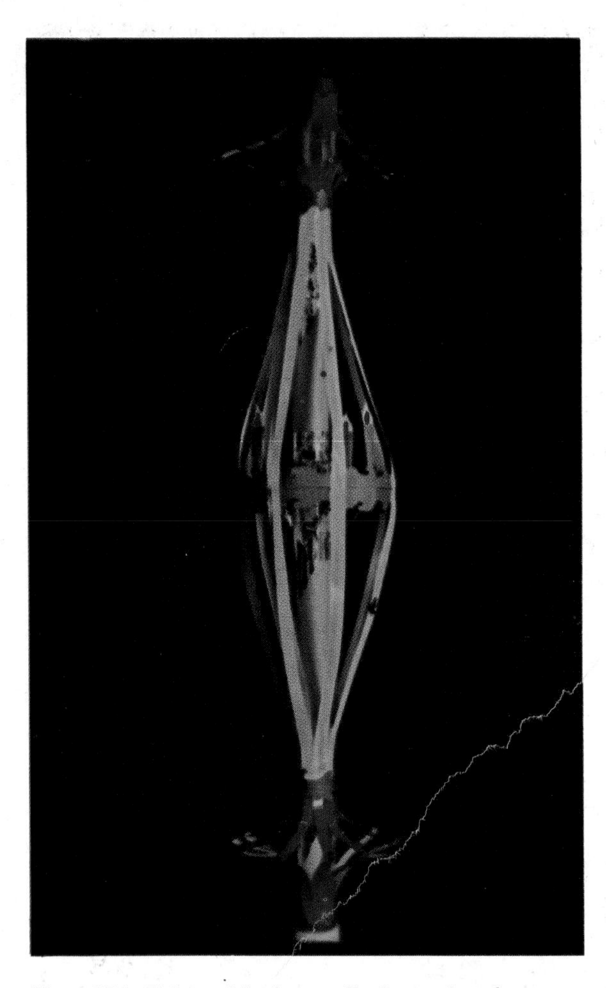

Illus. 174. This stabile has radiating strips that were not cut from a folded sheet of paper. Instead, individual strips are attached to the ends of the central tube. A strip of lavender paper was then inserted in the middle, its ends joined, and the strips glued to it so that they bell out. The lavender circle is held in place by the strips. Tiny, cylindrical paper candles with yellow flames are pasted to the central circle in the openings between the pink strips. Two small folded cylinders form the top and bottom sections.

Illus. 175. A wider cardboard tube forms the foundation for this stabile. Three separate and different-colored and different-shaped folded cylinders have been attached together to make very wide sections. Rectangular pieces of tagboard were sculptured into cylinders and then covered with tinfoil. These little shapes are joined to the central section by means of straight pins and give a merry-go-round effect to the finished stabile.

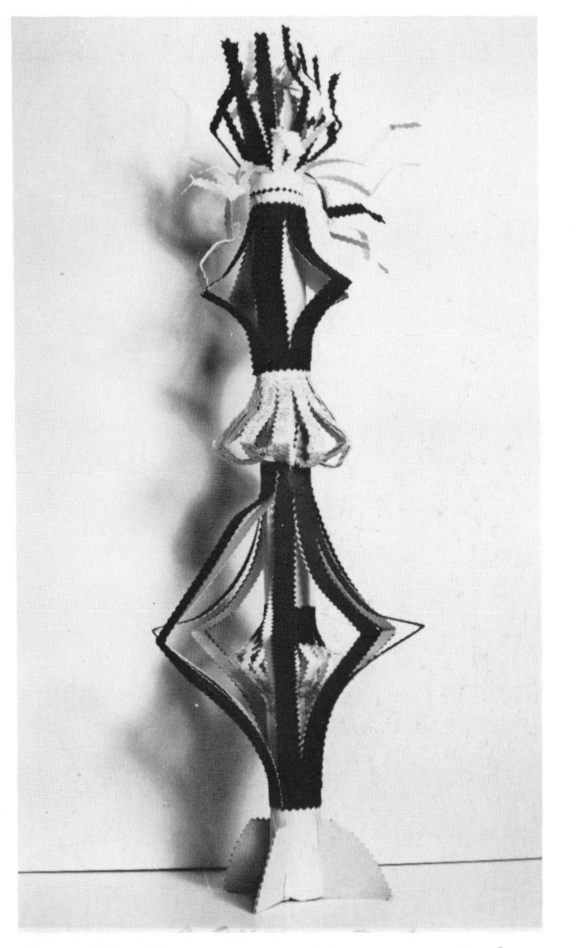

Illus. 176. These paper strips appear to be one color on the inside and another on the outside. This effect is achieved by cutting two pieces of different-colored construction paper together. A pinking shears made the irregular little notches along the edges of all of the paper parts.

Illus. 177. Following the same procedure of cutting folded pieces of paper, you can make a humanlike figure. Simply vary the sizes of the slits for each section as here where, for example, the head is formed from very widely spaced slits.

CYLINDRICAL LANTERNS AND MOBILES

Any of the stabiles you have made might also be used as mobiles. Try hanging one of your paper constructions from a single strand of nylon thread just below a ceiling light. Decorate it with glitter, bits of metallic foil, tinfoil, sequins or other shiny materials which will reflect artificial lights.

The paper cylinders in Illus. 166 through Illus. 170 might serve as decorative lanterns for a birthday party or other special occasion. For a holiday party, such as Christmas, you could make a lantern like the one in Illus. 166, but this time cut out recognizable Christmas symbols—bells, stars, angels, etc.

You might hang your lanterns over outdoor lights to add a festive touch to parties. If you do this, line the cut-out piece with colored transparent tissue paper or cellophane so that the light can shine through all of the openings.

CYLINDRICAL DECORATIONS

The central cores of the stabiles in Illus. 172 through Illus. 176 are more slender, making them more suitable for ceiling decorations. By placing a long string through the middle of the paper constructions so that they are lined up end to end, you can make party decorations by fastening one end of the string to the corner of the room and the other end to the ceiling light. If you attach one to each corner of the room, you will have a wonderfully festive atmosphere. For an added effect, string several together and hang vertically from both the corners and the ceiling light. These cylinders might be smaller than the horizontally hanging ones. Decorate them with a symbol of the occasion, such as paper turkeys, bunnies, etc.

Illus. 178. The cylinder form is ideal for body parts.

CYLINDRICAL PEOPLE

Can you name the number of cylindrical parts there are in the human body? Our arms and legs are, in a sense, composed of two cylinders each, as are our fingers. The torso and neck are both cylinders, and some people have long narrow heads that are somewhat cylindrical in shape. So, by using no other shape you can construct a human figure on this one geometric form.

The three figures in Illus. 178 are completely composed of paper cylinders. The Chinese laundryman is made of tagboard covered with pieces of colored tissue paper. Strips of tinfoil decorate the neck, sleeves and the front of his coat. The construction-paper policeman and Martian also have touches of tinfoil.

CYLINDRICAL MASKS

Using a cylinder you can make a mask that fits right over your head. The mask in Illus. 180

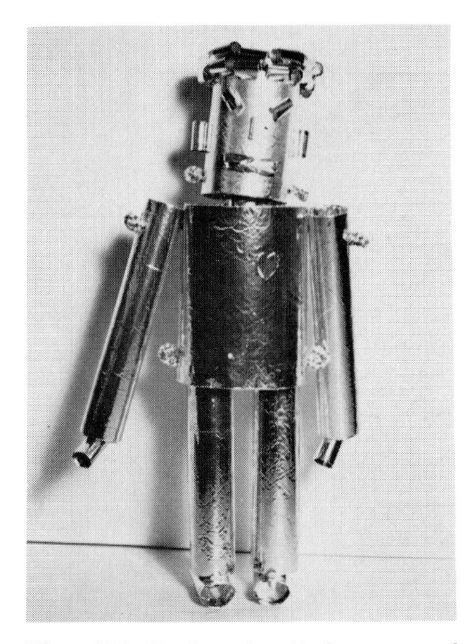

Illus. 179. Tagboard cylinders covered with tinfoil make a realistic robot. To hold the arms, legs, neck and head to the body, pipe cleaners have been inserted into each cylinder like pins. Little knots on the ends hold them in place.

has as its foundation a red construction-paper cylinder to which three-dimensional features have been added. The nose was cut out from a folded piece of orange construction paper, and folded paper ears support pipe-cleaner earrings. A single piece of chartreuse construction paper into which slits were cut and curled forms the beard. The fringed hairpiece was cut into diagonal slits, and his curly topknot is formed of long narrow strips of paper joined at their bases and then curled over a scissors' blade. A three-dimensional mouth was achieved by cutting tooth-like slits into the folded piece and bending them out.

Illus. 180. If you wear this mask, no one will know you! It fits right over your head, so that even your hair and neck are covered. A large construction-paper cylinder foundation and three-dimensional features provide you with a mask that will take a lot of wearing.

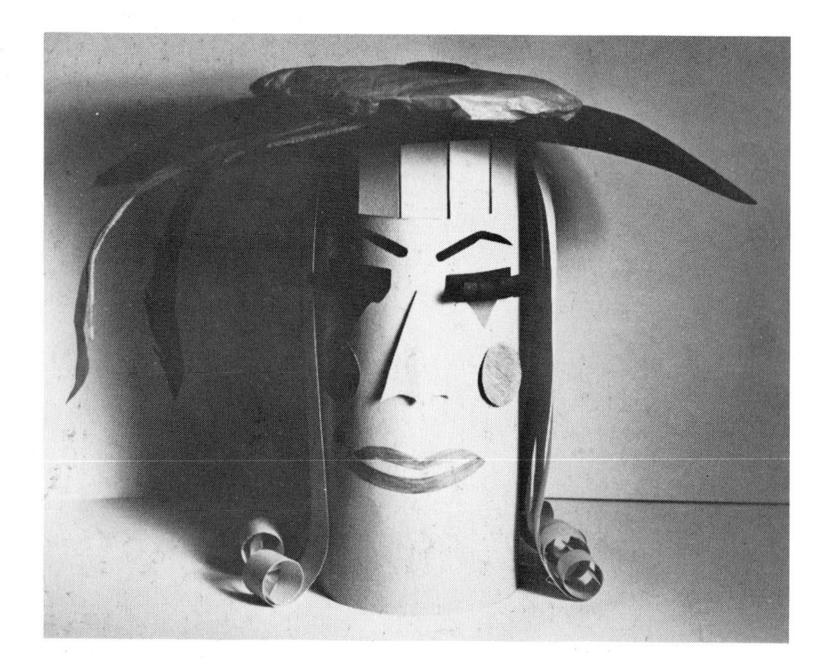

Illus. 181. Here is a fine mask for a costume party. The cylinder construction-paper head is crowned with a hat like a tissue-paper pillow. Crushed tissue has been covered by a single piece of tissue and glued to a large floppy construction-paper brim. Tissue-paper-covered pipe cleaners hang down like feathers. The lady's hair, a large sheet of paper, has slitted curls and bangs. Three-dimensional eye-lashes and nose, crayoned lips and paper-circle rouge spots make a sultry face.

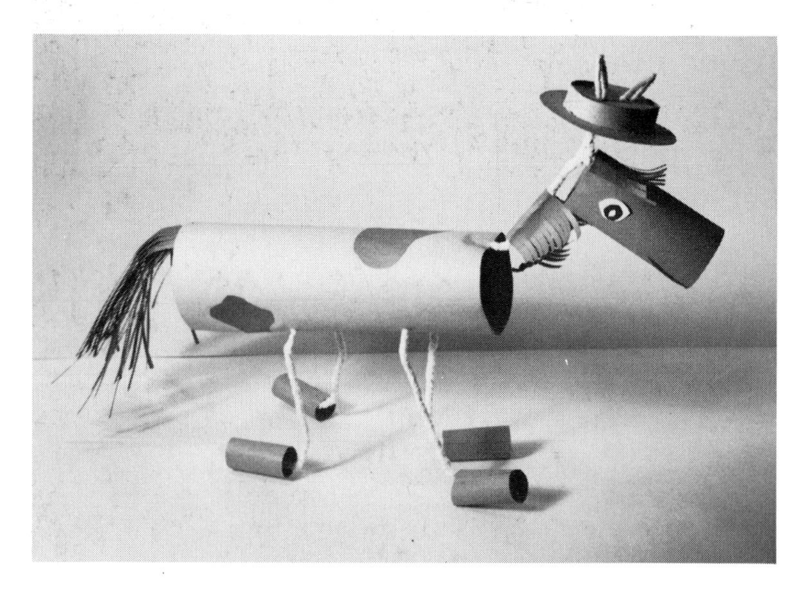

Illus. 182. This old Dobbin wears a tiny paper-sculptured hat which allows his pipe-cleaner ears to poke through. Another pipe cleaner joins his cylinder head to his body and is covered with a slitted-paper mane. His forelock and tail are composed of the same slitted construction paper. Small cylinder hoofs are connected to his tubelike body with taped-on pipe-cleaner legs. His wall-eye and spotted markings are made of various-sized and -shaped pieces of construction paper.

CYLINDRICAL CREATURES

Cows, horses, dogs, wild animals and birds all make ideal subjects for cylindrical constructions. The early bird who caught the worm in Illus. 183 is composed of two cylinders. Two long, 3-inch-wide strips of blue construction paper were sculptured into a head cylinder and a body cylinder, which were glued together. The two sections of the beak, holding the green crepe-paper worm, were formed from folded, triangular pieces of orange construction paper and decorated with yellow strips.

Two small circles of paper were cut into little spirals to form the three-dimensional eyes. The green, blue and orange feathers were cut from construction paper and then scored in the middle and pasted on to the body cylinders. Short blue fluffy paper shapes form the down on the bird's chest. Weblike feet, cut from orange construction paper, were glued directly on to the body, eliminating the need for legs.

A cylindrically shaped oatmeal carton forms the foundation of the winged creature in Illus. 184. A six-sided cardboard carton was taped to the body to form the head, and sections of a wire coat hanger, poked into the sides, make a frame for the wings. Paper strips of different colors were wound horizontally round the lower half of the body and slitted to suggest feathers. Yellow curled paper strips were glued one by one to the chest.

The tissue paper covering the wing frames has been brushed lightly with tempera paints to give them a feathery appearance.

Illus. 183.

Illus. 184.

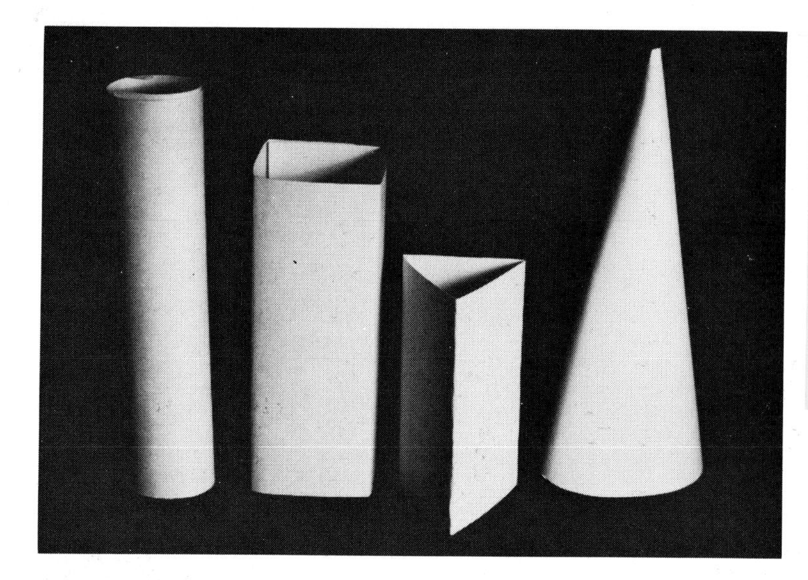

9. Combining Forms in Paper Sculpture

Illus. 185.

Just as the painter uses all the basic forms in one way or another to compose a picture, you will find that your experience in making the preceding projects will now lead you easily into combining them to form almost any conceivable object you wish. Since you haven't made any vehicles or buildings yet, let us start with a few simple means of transport, using basically the shapes shown in Illus. 185. The engine and boxcar in Illus. 186 might be a good starting project. Cones, cubes, cylinders are all used here. Notice the clever use of the cat-stairs as a coupling device.

Illus. 186. This engine and coal car display a variety of shapes—cylinders, cubes, cones and circles. A facial tissue rubbed in charcoal makes a nice pile of coal, overseen by a pipe-cleaner trainman.

Illus. 187. Another engine, this time hauling a caboose. Notice the variation on the cylindrical chimneys—the front one has an upside-down construction-paper cone. The roof of the caboose exhibits an interesting multi-levelled effect achieved by making several folds in a single sheet of paper.

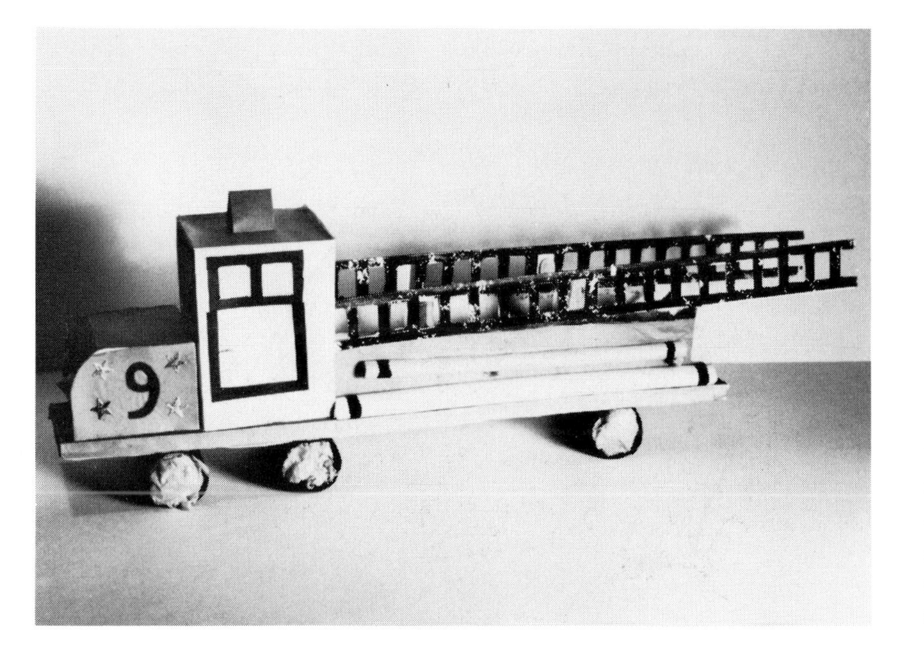

Illus. 188. A tagboard fire engine, covered with colored tissue paper, has a long paper cube base and a tri-cube body. Three paper cylinders stuffed with crushed tissue make roller-like wheels. The ladders are cut from tagboard and painted with black tempera.

Illus. 189.

Three paper cubes have been assembled to form the boxcar in Illus. 189. A wide, flat cube shape, approximately 1-inch thick provides a base upon which four construction paper wheels are attached by means of brass paper fasteners. The fasteners themselves resemble little hubs. The spokelike effect has been achieved by cutting out sections of a paper doily and pasting them on to the paper wheels. A cylinder chimney, topped by a cone, is constructed from colored metallic foil. See if you can make the little railing yourself.

If you would prefer to make an old-fashioned vehicle, why not try a covered wagon? A large paper cylinder resting on a cube base, which could have very large wheels attached to it, would provide you with the basic structure. Or you could make a frame for the top part with arched pipe cleaners. This frame might be covered with tissue paper. The cylindrical horses you made in Chapter 8 would make it even more realistic.

Antique cars with running boards and side trunks, aircraft of various types—helicopters, planes, blimps; boats—canoes, speedboats, tugboats—all can be fashioned from your basic paper sculptures.

Buildings of all kinds lend themselves well to combined forms. If you are ambitious, you could make an entire town with skyscrapers, factories, houses, churches and stores. Using a felt-tip pen, crayons or paints, brick, siding, or shingles could be added to the paper surfaces (see Illus. 190).

Illus. 190.

You could also use ready-made shapes such as cardboard cartons of various sizes and cover them with paper patterns that suggest window shutters, flower boxes, porches, gabled or hip roofs, or any other details you can think of. Then add sculptured people and animals. A farm would be an excellent project, too.

Although you cannot see it, the body of the little turkey in Illus. 191 is a construction-paper cylinder, encircled by two-dimensional paper rings with their middles cut out. Each of these rings is slitted to simulate feathers. The colorful, expandable tail is composed of four different-colored fans which are attached to the cylinder. An orange disk of paper forms the chest to which is joined a paper-strip head with a red wattle. Slitted wings and spiral eyes complete this whimsical bird.

The sad clown mask in Illus. 192 is composed of two large basic shapes—a cylinder and a cone. The paper cylinder is large enough to fit over the head. A small cone makes a fitting nose, and sheets of slitted, orange tissue paper provide our clown with a wild mop of hair. Shiny tinfoil teardrops and a turned-down construction-paper mouth convey his unhappy nature.

Illus. 191. A cylinder covered with paper rings makes up the body of this festive turkey.

Illus. 192. A cylinder head and a cone hat form the basic structure for an unhappy clown who is crying tinfoil tears.

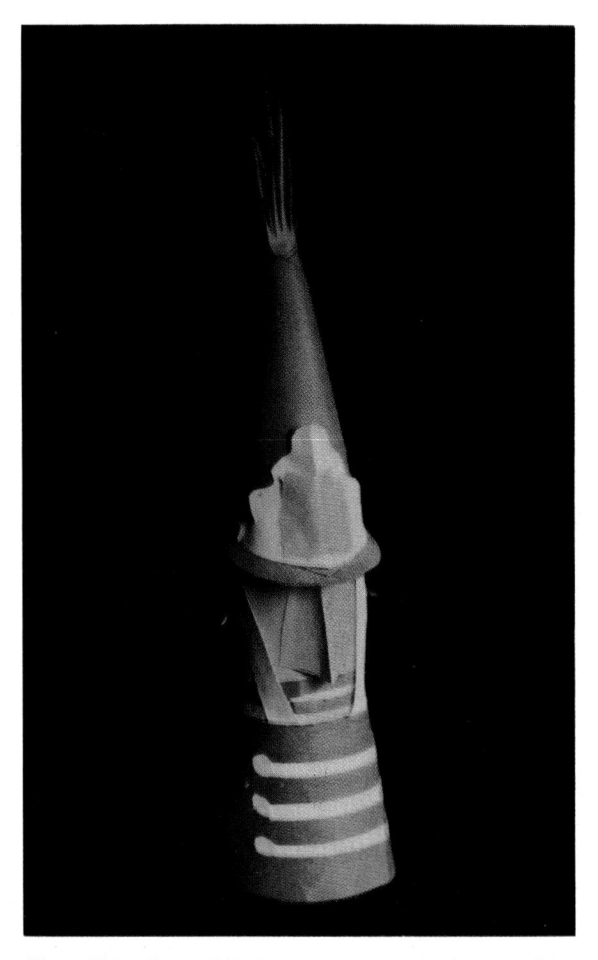

Illus. 193. This soldierly figure is ready for anything that might happen. A narrow paper cylinder topped by a cone helmet makes a very simple construction.

Illus. 194. A paper bumblebee is poised for flight.

One paper cylinder provides the smart looking cadet in Illus. 193 with a face and chest. A tall narrow cone makes his helmet which has a brim composed of a paper circle. Slitted blue construction paper suggests a feathery tuft. Regimental stripes of yellow run across his jacket. His strong, three-dimensional nose is a triangular piece of yellow paper folded in the middle.

The busy bee in Illus. 194 has a paper cylinder body covered with stripes of cast-off fur. Two shallow cones are placed at either end of the cylinder. A cat-stairs neck connects the tagboard cube head to the small front body cone. Another cone makes an effective stinger. The delicate wings are formed by tissue-paper-covered pipe cleaners. This bee is perched upon a wide cone base to which his six pipe-cleaner legs cling easily. Two other pipe cleaners form antennae.

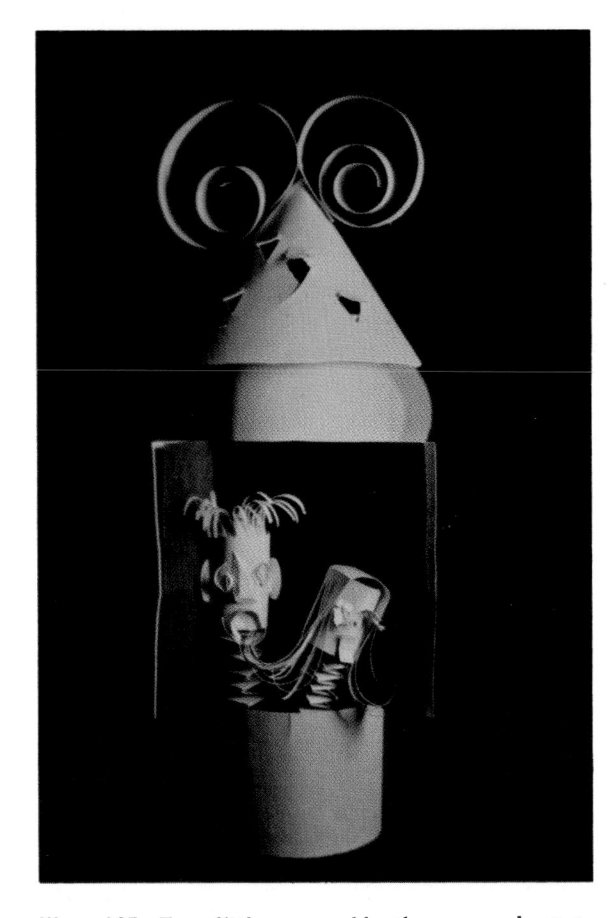

Illus. 195. Two little paper Martians are about to take off in their rocket ship for the open spaces. The cylinder and cone rocket has two doors that open. The spaceman on the left has a cylinder head and the one on the right a cube head. Both have cat-stairs bodies, three-dimensional eyes, noses, and mouths, and unruly slitted-paper locks.

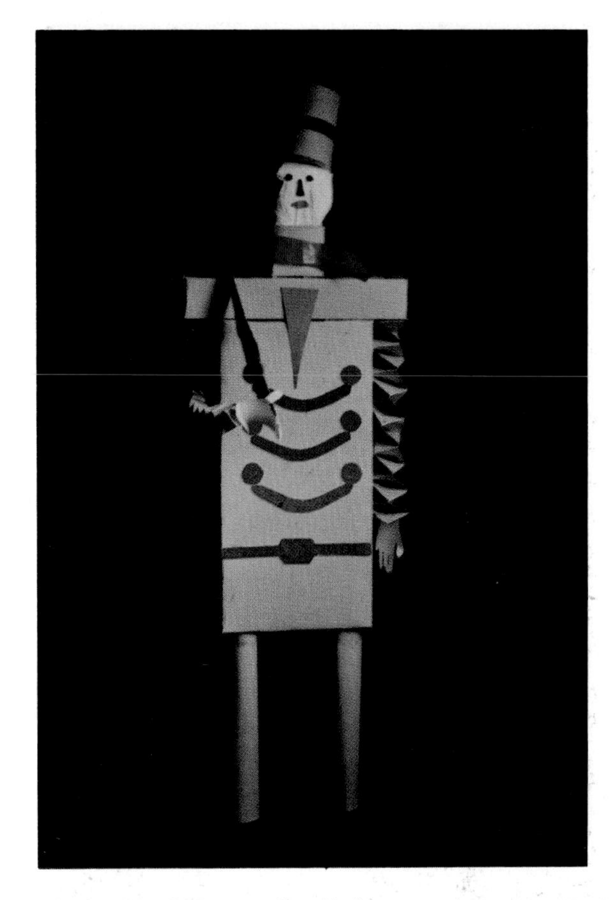

Illus. 196. Cubes and cylinders are important to this military man. His broad shoulders and his wide chest are cubical, and his neck, legs and hat are cylindrical. His cat-stairs arm holds a two-dimensional rifle, and flat pieces of paper serve as decorations. A ball of crushed tissue paper has been covered with white crepe paper to make a head.

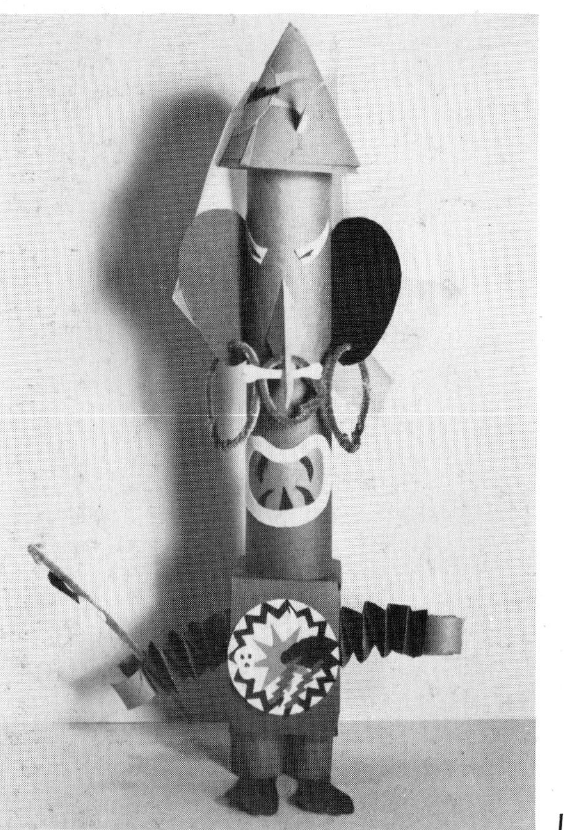

Illus. 197.

In Illus. 198 Goldilocks is trying out Baby Bear's chair. Her body consists of a large cone to which are attached two rectangular, folded legs. The base of the chair started out as a cube, from which sections were removed to make the rungs and legs. The chair back is cut from a flat sheet of paper and pasted to the base. Goldilocks' plastic foam head wears a cone bonnet from under which peep curly strands of yellow tissue-paper hair. Strips of lace trim the dress and hat, and small cubes form her feet.

Illus. 198.

Many of our geometric forms went into the making of the witch doctor in Illus. 197. A tall cylinder gives him a long narrow head, and two short cylinders provide stubby legs. In between he has a boxy cube body to which are attached wavy cat-stairs arms. A diamond-shaped piece of paper is folded once to create a three-dimensional nose, pierced by a paper bone and a pipe-cleaner ring. A cone-shaped headpiece rests above giant, floppy, pierced ears. Flat paper shapes provide features and decorative touches.

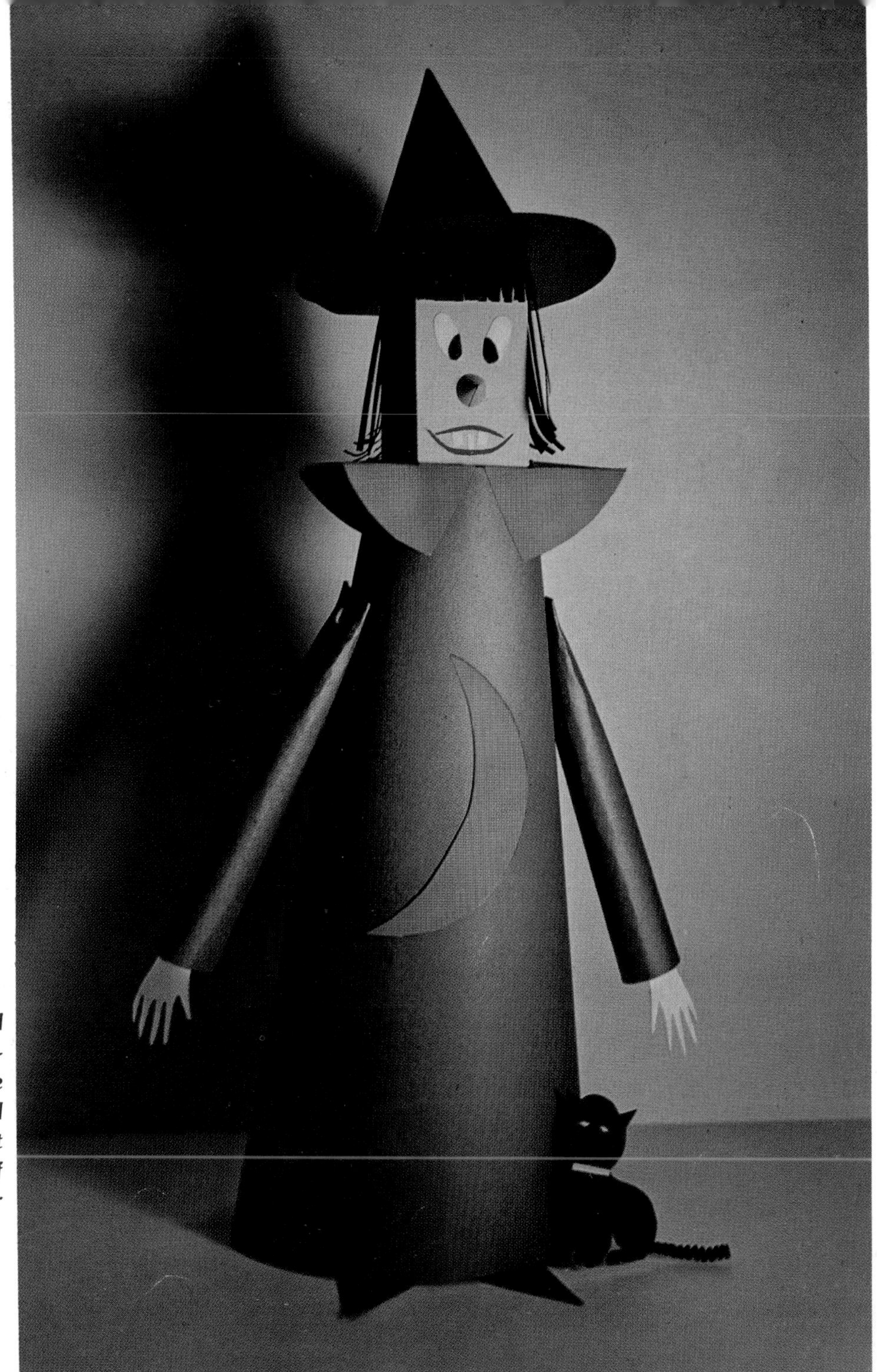

Illus. 199. Here is a Halloween witch and her black cat who don't need a broomstick or cauldrons to scare people. Three cylinders make her body and arms and a cube her head. Cones provide a hat and nose. Her unusual collar is made of two half circles of construction paper which are bent over on the ends.

Illus. 200.

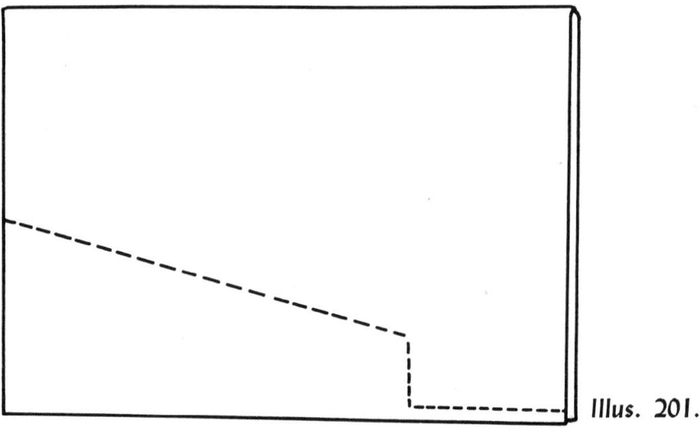

Illus. 201.

10. Paper Sculptured Flowers

Summer or winter you can have a gay potted bouquet of flowers to brighten up a drab area of a room. Three-dimensional paper flowers also make ideal Mother's Day presents. You might start by making a paper pot as shown in Illus. 200.

Fold a sheet of paper and lightly pencil on the lines shown in Illus. 201. Cut along these lines with the paper still folded and you will have a symmetrical, three-dimensional pot when you unfold it. Fold over the two tabs at the top of the pot and paste them to a sheet of background paper. However, you might wish to place the flowers in a basket instead of a pot. See Illus. 214 for basket ideas.

The blossoms in Illus. 200 were all made from paper cones. Illus. 202 shows the basic construction for these blossoms. Cut out several circles of different sizes. Make a slit directly to the middle of each ("A"). Overlap the edges slightly and paste together so that you have large shallow cones.

The small areas marked "B" in Illus. 202 indicate the cuts you can make to form petals. Sketch the petal shapes lightly on the circle, then cut them out. Although each blossom should have petals that are the same, try to vary the shapes of the petals from blossom to blossom. You can make deeper and narrower slits, very large ones, or very tiny ones. Think of the difference in the petals of a tulip from those of a daisy, for instance. (See page 113 for additional blossom suggestions.)

All flowers have "eyes" which are really the stamen. Some are long and frondy, others are short and cushionlike. In Illus. 203, we have constructed a pattern used in the top flower in Illus. 200 and which you might use to begin. Fold a piece of paper three times. Outline on the folded edge a small paddle shape. Cut it out, unfold and put the paddles together so that each rounded end is exposed. Pierce the middle with a brass fastener to hold them together and then poke it through the middle of your blossom. Spread the ends of the fastener on the reverse side to secure the "eye."

The tightly knit eye of the blossom at the lower left in Illus. 200 was made in a different way. A narrow piece of paper was slitted (Illus. 204) and then rolled tightly to form a cylinder (Illus. 205). A generous amount of glue was smeared on the bottom of the cylinder before attaching to the cone of the blossom.

The eye of the lower right blossom in Illus. 200 was made by cutting approximately 20 very narrow paper strips. One by one the strips were pierced with a brass fastener which was then pushed into the cone and the background paper. Then the strips were fluffed up and shuffled round to form the radial effect.

Leaves are simple to make. They can either be left flat or scored and folded, or you might curl them up with a scissors.

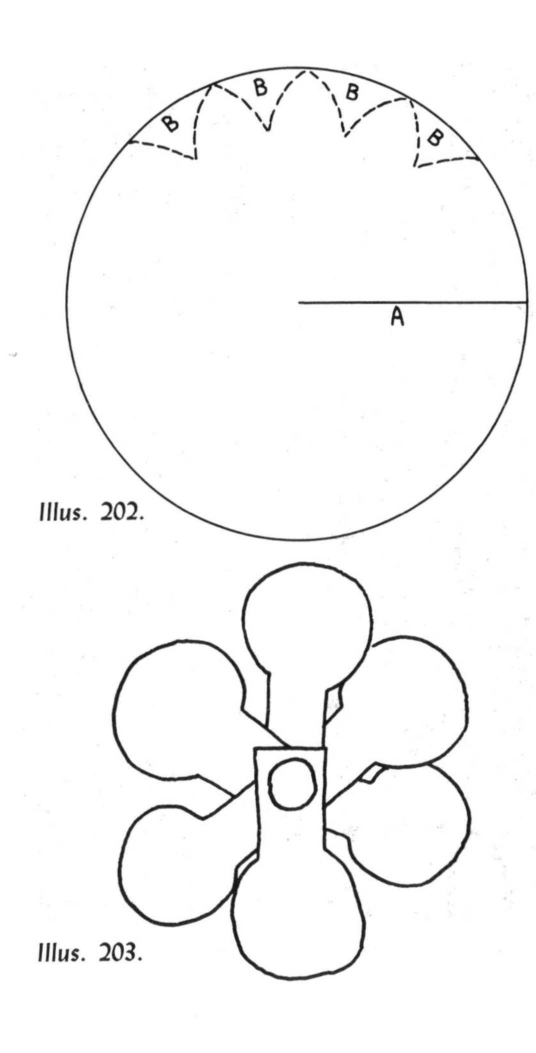

Illus. 202.

Illus. 203.

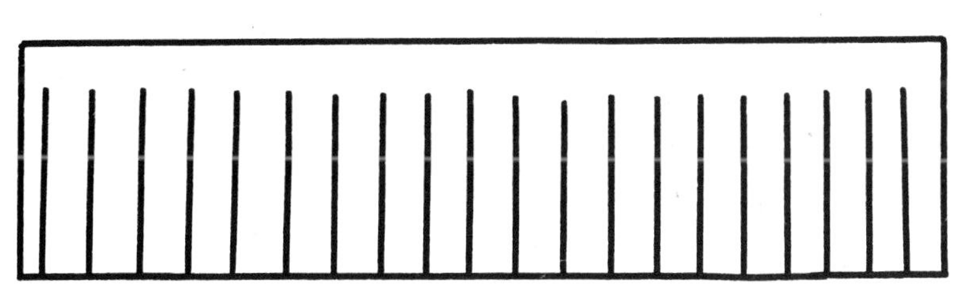

Illus. 204.

Illus. 205.

Illus. 206. Cones and strips form the blossoms in this flower arrangement. When attaching blossoms to the background paper, apply a generous amount of white liquid glue to the underside of the cone surrounding the point. Press against the background paper, at the same time flattening the point so that there is an adequate surface to hold the cone in place. Press until the glue has set.

Illus. 207. These calla-lily blossoms are not formed from perfect cones. When making the slit in the circle of paper, do not cut to the exact middle—cut somewhat to the left or right of the middle and you will have a rather lopsided cone.

Illus. 208. This bowl has a variety of blooms. The pink larkspur is made of tightly curled strips, while the other flowers are cone shaped, but each different from the other.

Illus. 209. The daisylike red flower at the lower right was made by folding narrow paper strips in the exact middle and fastening all the ends to the background paper with a brass paper fastener. The fastener is camouflaged under a tiny piece of green construction paper.

Illus. 210. The big yellow and orange bloom was constructed from two cones, one within the other. Some of the leaves, as you can see, are departures from the usual flat, scored ones you have been making. These three-dimensional leaves were formed from shallow fringed cones.

SOME BLOSSOM SUGGESTIONS

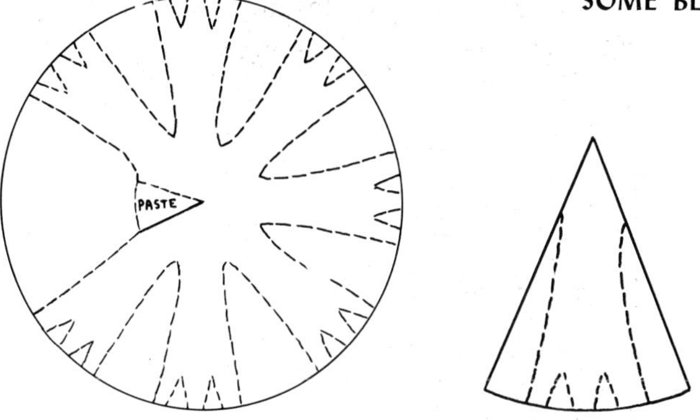

Illus. 211. To make this flower blossom, fold a circular piece of paper three times so that you have a triangular form as above. Cut out along the dotted lines. When you unfold you will have a design as at the left above. Cut one of the petals off, so that you can make your cone overlap easily.

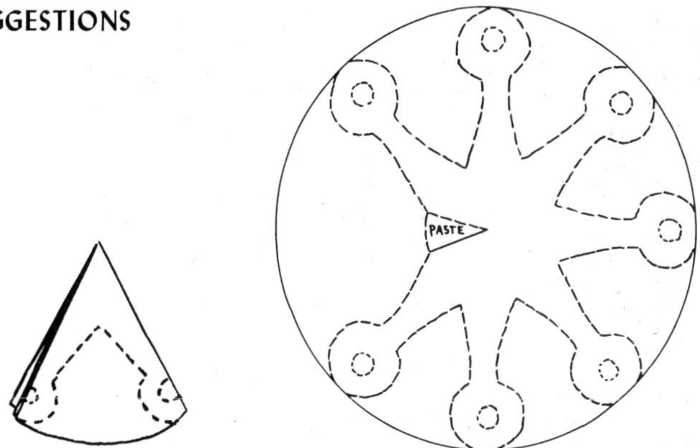

Illus. 212. This flower has paddlelike petals. Again fold a circular piece of paper three times and cut out as before.

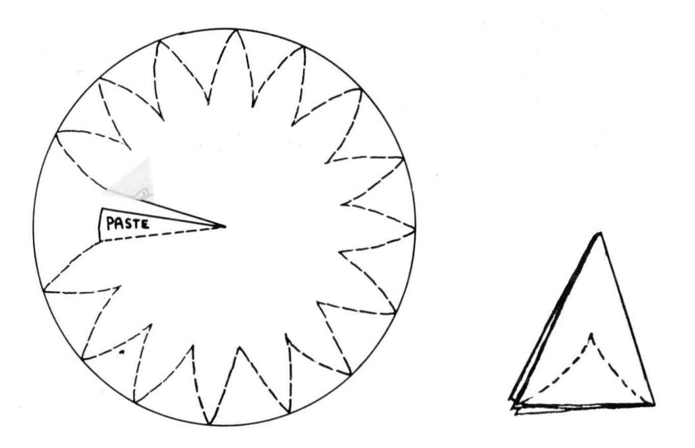

Illus. 213. This time fold your circle of paper four times and you will have a chrysanthemum type of bloom.

Illus. 214. If you would prefer not to paste your three-dimensional bouquets against a background, you might make a cone basket such as this one, using pipe cleaners for stems. Cubes and cylinders make good holders, too.

Illus. 215. At the far left, two large tri-cone flowers are united by construction-paper stems. Small triangular leaf shapes dot the background. On the right, cuplike cones are backed by half-moon circles. Paper insects hover over the blossoms.

Illus. 216. The daisylike blossoms at the far left are composed of cones within cones. Tiny paper strips make the stamen and the slivers hanging off the edges of the petals. On the right, each blossom is made up of two side-by-side cones, one slightly larger than the other. Here is an example of a lopsided cone achieved by making a slit into the paper circle from the edge to a point some distance from the exact middle.

Illus. 217. These two arrangements show the great variety of shape you can achieve with the simple cone.

Imaginative flower forms and colors make up the arrangements in Illus. 217. In the upper section, three yellow cones form the blossom bases. The ruffled, petallike effect was achieved by making several creases from the edge to the middle of each cone.

The eyes are formed of smaller, orange cones which are poked through the middle of the blossom by means of a paper fastener. Small strips of paper radiate from the middle of each eye. The orange and black strips on the yellow cones add a decorative touch.

The leaves of orange and blue placed behind the three large blossoms serve to continue the radiating movement from the central axis. The leaves, instead of being scored and folded down the middle, have narrow black strips that simulate a central crease.

The lower panel in Illus. 217 shows a subdued harmony of color with blues of various shades making up the total color scheme against the black background. Each blossom has a central cone with little paper-strip stamen. Four rounded, light-blue petals, bordered in darker blue, rest underneath each flower. Radiating, light-blue leaves with a dark-blue stripe and a light-blue border complete the composition.

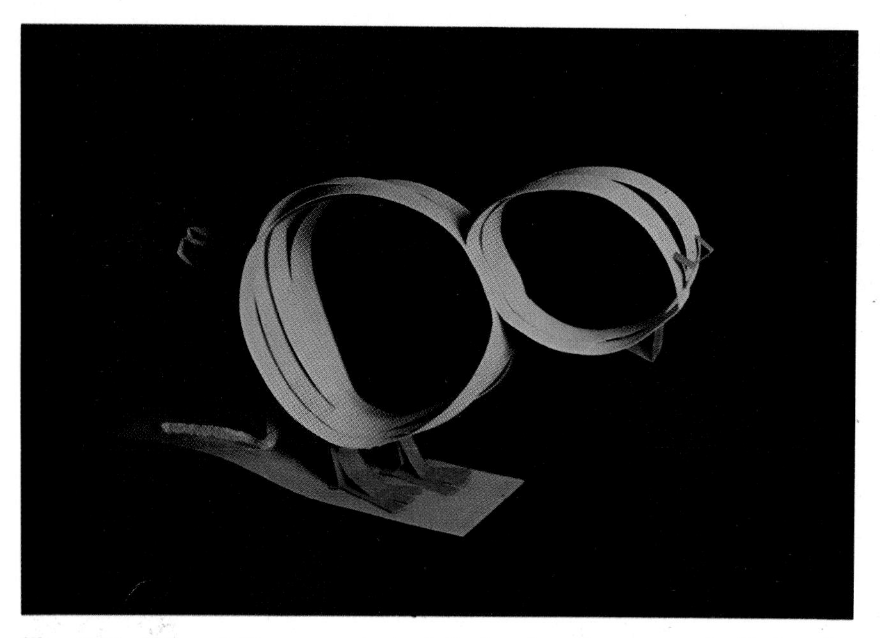

Illus. 218. Although it appears to be full already, this paper-strip bird on its strip of grass is ready to seize the next worm which happens by.

Illus. 219.

11. Paper Strip Sculpture

Another way to experiment in three-dimensional paper design is to limit yourself to using paper strips of varying length, as shown in Illus. 219. You can create free-standing sculptures of all sorts of figures, both imaginary and realistic, by combining paper strips in various ways. Paste, cellophane tape, or staples can be used to attach the strips together, and using strips of different colors will help you to add interest to your figures.

In Illus. 218, a small circle of strips placed side by side was attached to a larger circle to form the head and body of a bird. Two fat orange strips were

Illus. 220. A strange-looking bird with a long flat beak is ready to grab the worm also.

Illus. 221. Brown strips outline the masts and body of the ship, yellow and white define the sails, and dark blue wavy strips suggest the water. All are placed against a light blue sky to make a lovely study in color as well as composition.

pasted on the larger circle to form the bird's feet, and one on the smaller circle for its beak. Two curled strips make a tail, and, with two little blue tufts of feathers, the figure is complete. To help it stand, a pipe cleaner is glued to the back of the circular body and then bent to run along the paper base. The more active bird which is nosing its way along in Illus. 220 was made essentially the same way. The head, a strip which has been shaped into a teardrop, is joined to an oval-shaped body. Its full tail is made up of wide, different-colored strips which have been curled, and its legs are paper strips reinforced with pipe cleaners to help it stand. A pipe cleaner has been glued to the inside of the paper-strip body also, to keep it from collapsing under the weight of the feathers. The two on its head are for decorative effect.

RELIEF PICTURES

Your awareness of color, shape and design will grow when you bend your efforts towards making relief pictures. These pictures, such as the ship in Illus. 221 and the sailboat on the following page, are "drawn" with construction-paper strips—bending, angling and curving them as if they were crayon lines. The strips stand out from the back-

Illus. 222.

Illus. 223. A self-portrait which has been sculptured by a young artist.

ground when they are attached to it by one edge. The attaching can be done a number of ways. The simplest is to use transparent tape. Or small paper tabs, the same color as the background, might be bent and glued on to the background and the inside of the paper strips. If you do not want the paper tabs to show at all, you can cut small slits in the background with a razor, slip the tabs through, and glue them to the back of the picture.

In Illus. 222 (opposite page), a sailboat has been drawn with paper strips. Just a few are needed to give the outlines of sail, mast and body of the boat. The red strip suggests a tiller, a few blue strips the waves and a yellow circle with radiating strips makes the sun. The pink background gives the feeling of catching a glimpse of the craft at either dawn or sunset.

Portraits can be an absorbing subject for relief pictures. In Illus. 223, the strips outline a girl's head very effectively, and the shadows cast by the three-dimensional outline give the figure added interest.

Animal shapes can be tried in relief also, as shown in Illus. 225 on the following page. If you get very ambitious, you can try combining several objects or figures together to make a scene. Remember that angled paper strips give a different feeling than curved ones, and that the combination of the two will make your picture more interesting.

Illus. 224. A lovely angel, whose paper-strip body is attached to one strip which forms its base. A single strip was wound many times around a finger to make the head, and the wings are four looped strips attached to the neck. Christmas glitter gives the angel an ethereal touch.

Illus. 225. A cheerful rooster, artfully "drawn" with blending red and green strips.

Relief pictures can also be highly successful as abstracts. By varying the shapes and widths of the paper strips, as well as their colors, you can create exciting designs. Using different materials for the background will help too. The effect of your design can be greatly enhanced by placing it against tissue paper, newsprint, subdued wallpaper or translucent paper materials.

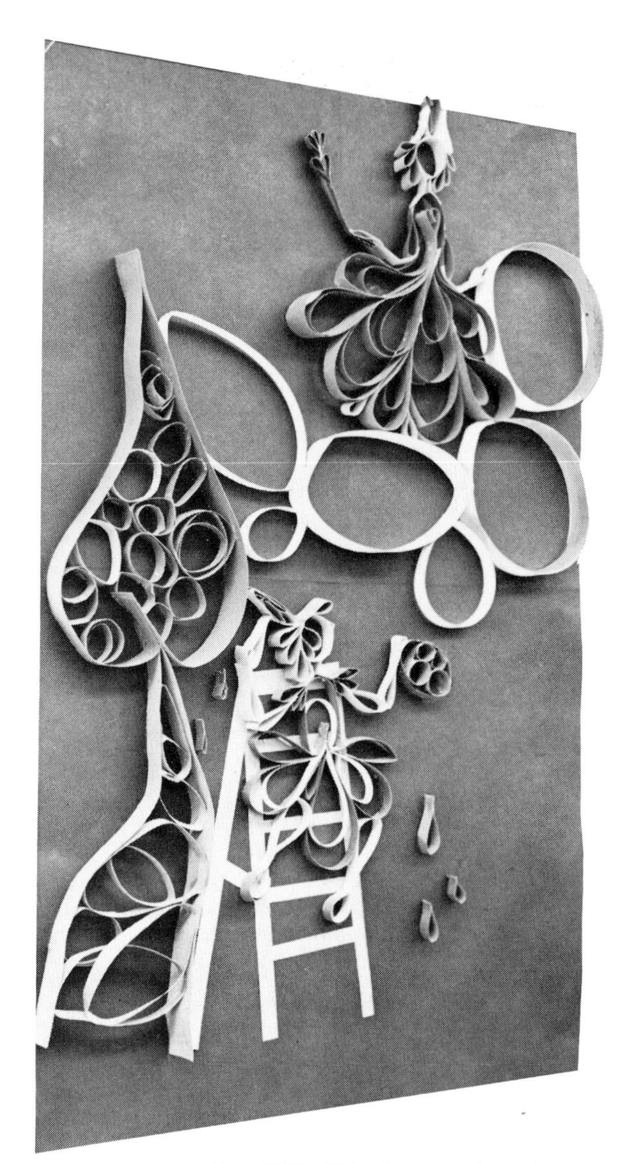

Illus. 226. This is a version of some of the objects from "Alice in Wonderland." The ladder is the only flat drawing, which emphasizes the three-dimensional quality of the others.

Illus. 227.

Illus. 227 shows an abstract design in which the paper strips vary in both width and shape, and are placed so that they vary in depth as well. Circles, teardrops, ovals and spirals are placed beside and within each other to create a lovely composition. The background of this design is a bulletin board, its color showing through the spaces outlined by the strips. Around the board is a black cardboard frame, which gives the picture a finished look.

The large clown in Illus. 228 has been done by combining paper circles of different sizes with a few wavy strips for the balloons' strings. Some of the circles have been filled in with colored tissue paper to give variety to the figure. The clown is attached to a background of semi-transparent, textured paper.

This design was exhibited against a glass door, and when the light shone through, the texture of the translucent background, the semi-transparent tissue paper, and the opaque construction-paper strips all came to life to create an unusual pattern.

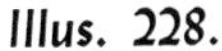

Illus. 228.

In Illus. 229 on the following page, circles of different sizes were again combined, this time to form the leaves of a tree. The dark construction-paper strips are placed against a white background for contrast.

Another way to experiment in paper-strip sculptures is to make mobiles with the figures you create, as shown in Illus. 230.

Illus. 229. A graceful tree, made by combining circles and lines. If you look closely at its middle you will discover a partridge there, with little circles forming the tufts of the bird's head and another group of circles its tail.

Illus. 230. A descending line of birds floats gracefully through the air. Curled and bent paper strips have been stapled together to form the mobile. Three curled strips placed on each head form their tufts, and curled pieces sprout from behind to suggest tails. Different-colored sheets of tissue paper fill in between the curved strips to make the bodies. The bars of the mobile were made with balsa wood—threads connect the birds to the bars.

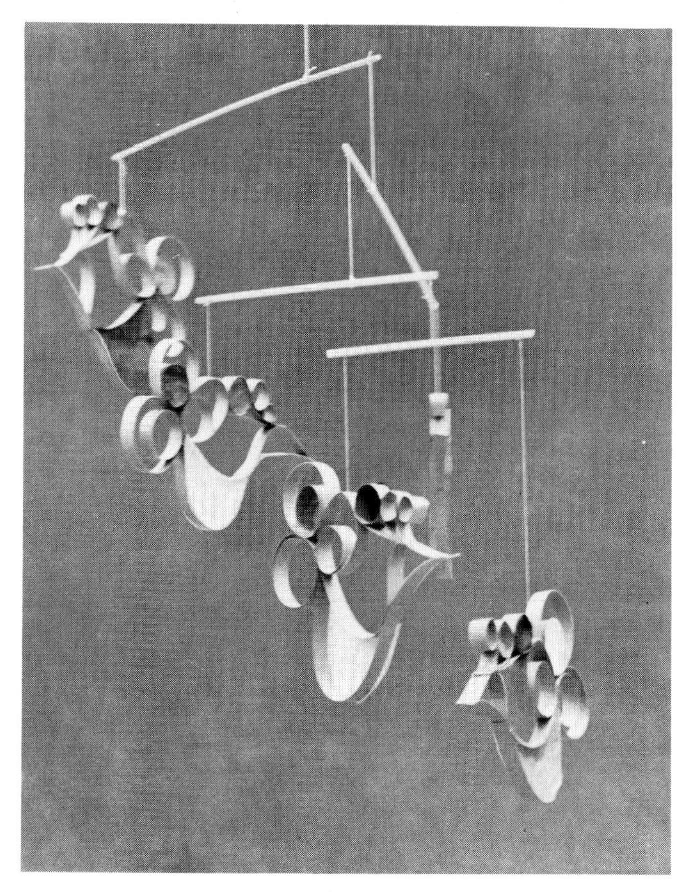

PAPER STRIP HATS

A delightful way to explore paper-strip sculpture and add to your wardrobe at the same time is to make hats with paper strips. You could make it a social affair by inviting friends to a hat-making party, including a fashion show at the end of it to model your new creations.

To begin a hat join the ends of a paper strip, or of two attached strips, into a circle which fits comfortably around your head. The width of the

Illus. 231. A tilted flag waves gaily from the top of the patriotic hat, attached by means of a red pipe cleaner. The blue and white strips are gathered at the top of the crown and attached there. Silver glitter has been scattered on the blue square of the flag to suggest stars, and a wavy line of glitter on the red headband gives the hat an added gaiety. This one is just right for a parade!

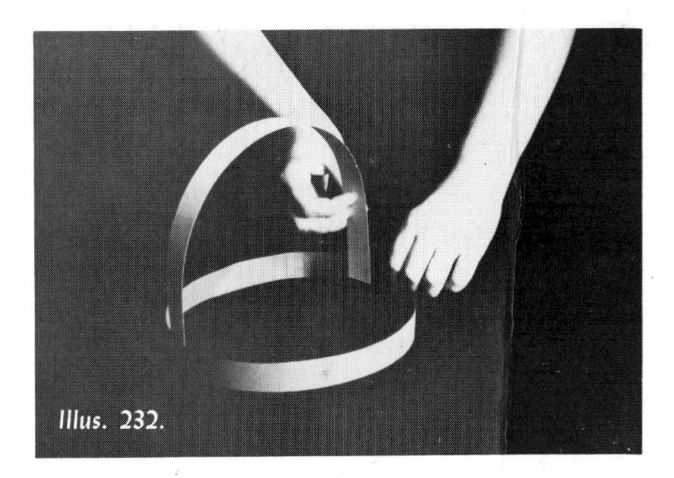

Illus. 232.

strip will depend on how wide you want the band of your hat.

Attach a paper strip to the inside of the band and loop it before attaching to the opposite side (see Illus. 232). As in the paper-strip sculpturing previously described, you can use staples, glue, rubber cement or paste to attach the strips. Now, working around the band, attach in the same manner even strips an equal distance apart. The result is shown in Illus. 233.

Illus. 233.

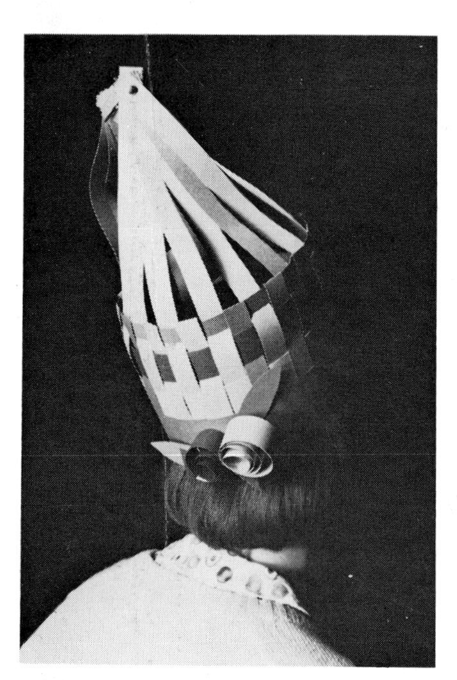

Illus. 234.

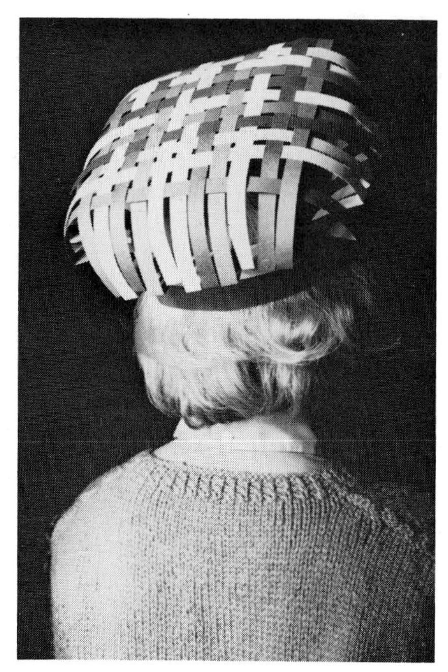

Illus. 235.

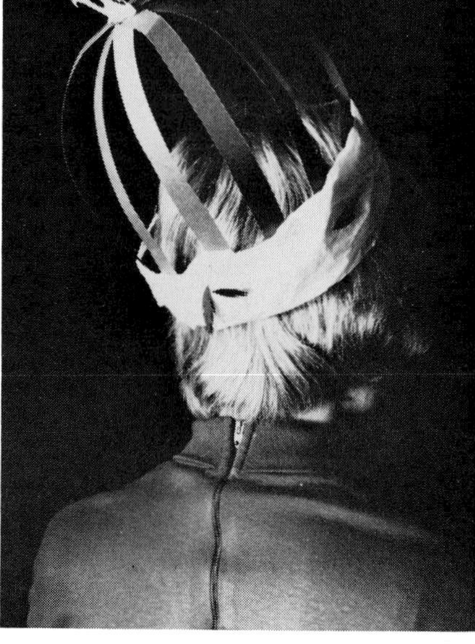

Illus. 236.

The loops of the hat in Illus. 234, like those of the patriotic hat on the preceding page, are not rounded and glued to both sides of the band. Instead, each strip extends vertically upward, and one brass paper fastener, by holding all the ends together, forces each strip to slant towards the middle of the crown. This hatband is a wide one with a checkerboard design, the result of three horizontal strips of paper having been woven alternately across the vertical strips. Two curled strips and two flat ones are combined to suggest a flower at the back of the hat.

The hat in Illus. 235 is a completely woven one. Blue, white and yellow strips were looped across and attached to opposing inner sides of the band to form the loom.

Illus. 237.

Strips of the same colors were then woven across the loom and also attached to opposing inner sides of the band. When this young lady gets tired of wearing her hat, she can turn it over and use it as a basket!

Illus. 236 shows a hat which resembles a bird cage. Its top has a little figure perched on it, and for a unique decorative touch, tissue paper has been wrapped around and attached to the band. Small pieces of dark paper have been glued to the tissue to give the impression that the headband is made of ermine fur.

The fetching cap in Illus. 237 was begun by using two circles instead of one. Paper strips of different colors were glued to the inside of the larger, lower circle. They were then bent outward before being glued to the inside of the smaller circle which rests on the top of the head. Short strips were glued to the lower inside of the larger circle and bent to radiate outward. Longer strips were joined to the smaller circle to make a decorative touch, and with a draped bow attached to the left lower side, the cap is complete. See if you can guess what she used to cut the strips, to give the hat its frilly effect.

While many hats look like bird cages, the one in Illus. 238 actually is one, although its bars are wide enough to allow the bird to escape if it wishes. Two orange strips are looped in a criss-cross and attached inside the pink headband. Silver glitter is pasted on them for a decorative effect. A pipe cleaner is poked through the top of the hat, where the "bars" cross.

Illus. 238. This hat of many colors is unique because it draws interest to the inside as well as the outside. The outside silver glitter along the orange strips gives an extra embellishment to the already sprightly head covering. When the hat is moving, the bird and branch swing back and forth, the curlicues bob up and down, and the flower on the top sways in all directions.

Illus. 239.

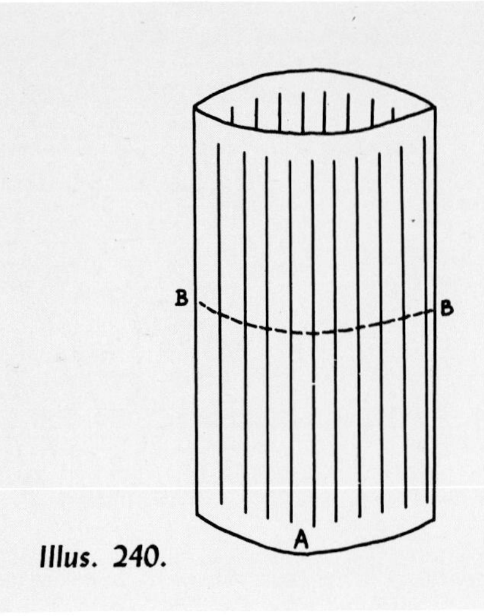

Illus. 240.

The elaborate hat pictured in Illus. 239 was begun the same way that the previous ones were—a paper band, cut from construction paper, was fashioned into a circle. Petal-shaped paper strips were then attached to the inside of the headband and bent to radiate down and outward. These strips were cut from construction and wrapping paper. If you look closely you will see the designs on some of the strips.

In order to make the main body of the hat, a sheet of construction paper was folded in half and slits were cut across it (perpendicular to the fold), ending 1 inch from the edges opposite the fold. The paper was unfolded and turned so that the cut slits ran vertically, and then joined together so that it made a cylinder (see Illus. 240). The lower rim of the cylinder (A) was fitted into the headband and pasted around the band's inner side, and a horizontal strip of tissue paper then wound around the middle of the cylinder (B) where the fold was, as a result of cutting the slits. The tissue-paper strip was drawn in tightly, gathering the vertical strips in together and creating two halves in the main body of the hat.

A circle of construction paper was next placed on top of the upper end of the cylinder. This gave a surface on which the hat designer could place many flowers of different sizes, shapes and colors. The flowers were cut from construction and tissue paper, and glued to pieces of fine wire. Each piece of wire supports one petal, and the wires are twisted together to form the flowers' stems. The blossoms were attached not only to the top of the hat but to its sides as well by poking the wires into the vertical slits and running them along the inside of the hat. Because the flowers move when the wearer walks, the hat gives the impression of a flower garden being invaded by a gentle breeze.

Start with a vertically slit cylinder yourself, and see what you can do with it. You can use pipe

cleaners instead of wire to hold objects on to the side of your hat. A short, fat cylinder will give a different effect than a tall, slim one.

The hat in Illus. 241 is unusual because it has nothing rising above the headband. The band itself is colorfully colored with small circles which have been cut out of tissue paper or else crayoned on. Two rows of paper strips form the body of the hat. The upper row of green strips was pasted on the inside of the band first, and the yellow row second. In the green row the ends of three strips are pasted together, and in the lower row ends of two are attached. The same kind of scissors was used to cut these strips as that used in Illus. 237.

The head covering in Illus. 242 is perfect for a comic figure in a play or pantomime! Purple and green strips are woven to make the flat crown, the ends of the strips being pasted against the inside of the purple headband. A ring of green construction paper was put around the band for the brim, and strips of orange paper were glued to the lower inside of the purple headband to make a

gay wig. The strips are straight for the bangs and slightly curled for the rest of the hair. A tall daisy is this hat's chief decoration. The two leaves and stem are attached to pipe cleaners for support, and the yellow paper blossom is given petals by cutting slits down to its middle.

The interesting headgear in Illus. 244, a variation of a straw hat, contains two woven areas. The one on the crown of the hat was made by first pasting vertical strips on the inside of the headband.

Illus. 244.

Eventually they are gathered to the middle of the crown, just as was done previously in Illus. 242. Also like Illus. 242, horizontal strips are woven across the vertical ones before they are gathered.

Illus. 245.

This time, however, the strips are circles which are woven flat across the crown rather than in a rounded fashion, to give the straw-hat effect. A ribbon of many bows, made with small loops of construction-paper strips, was fastened to the gathered ends of the vertical strips by means of a brass paper fastener.

Next, short strips were pasted to the lower inside of the headband and bent slightly to radiate outward. Three more horizontal rings of alternating strips were woven across the short strips to give the flat brim. Notice that the crown has been woven into a checkerboard pattern, while the pattern of the brim is that of stripes up to the edge, where the effect of the checkerboard occurs again.

Our last suggestion for paper-strip sculpture is that of the basket of fruit, in Illus. 245. The basket was made by weaving strips of different colors together. Three layers of blue strips were looped across the top and joined to the basket at both ends by brass paper fasteners to make the handle. (You can see by now that the paper fasteners can be extremely helpful to you!) More strips were then wrapped around the long horizontal ones to give the handle a finished look.

Strips of the same color, and even in length, were fastened together at both ends. They were then fanned out around tissue paper of the same color and approximate shape of the fruit. The grapes are the result of attaching several purple, curled strips to a brown central stem. Flat leaves and stems on some of the fruits complete the composition, which is indeed a feast for the eyes.

These are only some of the ways to work with paper strips. By experimenting you can discover many variations in areas discussed, and perhaps find new areas of your own.

12. Paper Bag Sculpture

MASKS

A paper bag can be transformed from a mundane, drab receptacle into an object of art with a touch of crayon and imagination. Its oblong depth makes it an ideal basic shape for a mask. By slipping it over your head before you start to draw on it and marking the areas of your eyes, nose and mouth, you'll have the starting points for your mask. You can then either cut these areas out or paint them on.

Illus. 247.

Illus. 246.

To the basic shape of the paper bag you can add horns, large or small ears, all sorts of noses, eyelashes, a beard, a mustache, and so on. Look about for some scrap materials and see what they suggest to you. You can use tempera paint, chalk or crayon to make your designs.

The smiling face which seems to be gazing downward in Illus. 246 has been painted with yellow, orange and red tempera. Both its colors and flowing lines give the visage an Indan look, and the lines continue to flow on to the red construction-paper ears. Notice the graceful shape of the eyes, which have been integrated into the pattern. A

(Above) Illus. 249. Two yellow cones make the horns for this mask, balanced by two longer yellow cones which form tusks. Notice the lower row of teeth along its chin!

(Left) Illus. 248. A bold design of many colors helps to make this face a fierce one. The artist has varied his brush strokes also, to make an interesting surface area.

diamond-shaped piece of paper has been folded vertically and attached for a nose, while the mouth has been painted on. The mask is topped with curly yellow hair, as a result of attaching two sheets of yellow construction paper cut into fat, bending strips.

The appealing paper-bag fellow in Illus. 247 on page 129 has red ears made from tagboard, pierced with colored pipe cleaners. The raised eyebrows are also made with pipe cleaners. Huge eyes are cut from black construction paper, with little strips to form the eyelashes. A macabre effect is given to the face by attaching a red cylinder for its nose, giving it black paper teeth, from which a red tongue gaily protrudes.

How would you like to unexpectedly face the face in Illus. 248? His wild, unruly hair—made with excelsior—and his crossed eyes give him a ferocious look which is aided by huge, menacing teeth. A drinking cup was used for his nose, and a paper "bone" was placed under it for added effect. Large paper ears, painted with the same design as that used for the colorful face have been attached.

Two slits, each about 3 inches long have been cut on both sides of the paper bag to allow its owner to fit the mask well over his shoulders. The front of the bag then drapes down to form a beard. The back of the bag could also drape down as long hair.

A no less ferocious face is shown in Illus. 249. The mouth of the preceding mask now seems quite tame in comparison to that of this one. The corners of the mouth are turned grimly downward, and two enormous teeth jut out of it and over the nether lip, sharpened for action! His triangular-shaped eyes give him an evil look, and the impression that he could frighten any evil spirits which happened his way.

Yellow, black and orange shapes—mainly triangular—have been combined in a geometric pattern which resembles that of Indians or Eskimos. Notice how balanced both colors and shapes are.

In just these four masks, a wide range of expression and feeling has been presented. See what *you* can do now to present yourself differently to the world.

Illus. 250. A boy puts the finishing touch on a monster which he has created. Its body is made of two stuffed bags which have been joined together, and it has no less than six arms and two beaks—all made of construction paper. Pipe cleaners make effective claws, as well as horizontal antennae. Wallpaper, doilies, and a partial paper plate decorate the figure's surface, making the monster quite a civilized one.

Illus. 251. Adding a red wattle gives the turkey a realistic touch. See Chapter 15 for more ideas on three-dimensional patterns you can use on your paper-bag animals.

CREATURES

A more ambitious project with a paper bag is to make an animal or bird. You can stuff the bag with crushed paper to give the animal's body solidity, as was done for the stolid, dignified turkey in Illus. 251. The end of the bag was gathered and tied with string, and then flattened into a fan shape. The fan then served as a foundation for the turkey's tail. Colored paper feathers were glued to the fanned end, radiating upward into a tail that any turkey would be proud to own.

A two-dimensional paper head has been attached to the flat bottom of the bag, and a large wing has been placed on either side of the body. Two sturdy cylinders for its legs are placed on flat webbed feet. Small triangular slits have been cut around the bag and bent slightly outward to suggest feathers, with glitter sprinkled on to highlight them.

PUPPETS

A greatly rewarding project is to make puppets with paper bags of all sizes. You can either make unique ones with which to entertain your friends, or create a whole cast of characters and put on a show. The variety of decorative materials is endless; paper doilies, buttons, ribbon, glitter, wallpaper patterns, cotton batting, tongue depressors, broom bristles, artificial flowers, rug filler, scouring pads, netting, wood shavings, notebook rings and so on.

There are two basic ways in which the paper bag can be used to form the head. As shown on the left of Illus. 252, the eyelids can be drawn on the lower flap of the bag's bottom. The eyes are then drawn directly underneath the flap, so that when the flap is down, the little figure has its eyes shut, and when the flap is up, the puppet has its eyes open.

The second way, as the figure on the right

Illus. 252.

Illus. 253. Bodies, made with flat sheets of paper, have been added to the heads shown in Illus. 252 to make a charming couple. She has been decorated with two large doilies on the back of her head, and he has been given a large bow tie.

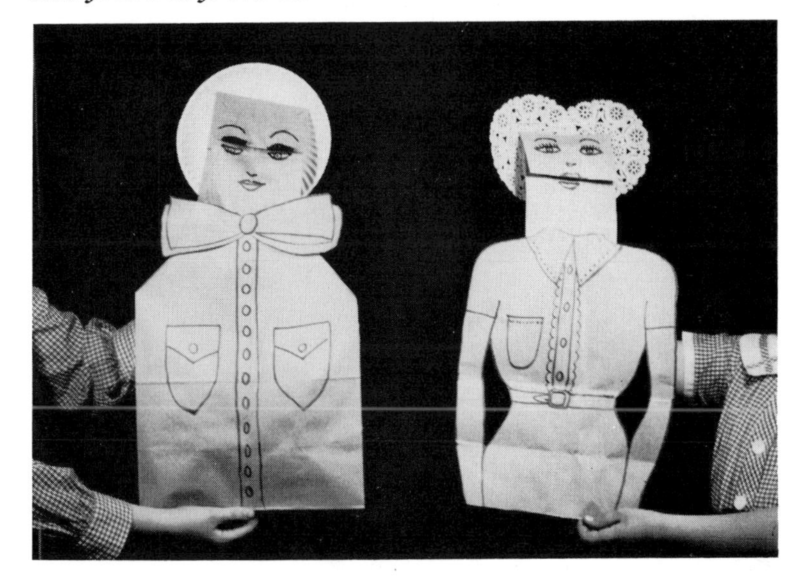

Illus. 254. This fellow who looks about to speak has been gaily decorated with tempera paint, and strands of yarn make interesting hair. The puppet's large bow tie is made out of crepe paper, and his striped shirt out of wallpaper.

Illus. 255. The children gather at a table on which tempera paints of various colors have been put. Notice the round-eyed look of the puppet on the far right—pipe cleaners encircle small black buttons. The pipe cleaners also make an effective mustache.

Illus. 256. Round eyes are now gazing in all directions as a group of children work on their puppets, with the one from Illus. 255 in the middle. Look closely and you'll find the monster from Illus. 250 in the crowd.

If you want to represent the character from its waist up, you can stuff a larger bag and attach it to the head bag in order to give the puppet a body. If you join it to just the front side of the head bag, you can still put your hand inside the head to manipulate the eyes or mouth.

If you want to give the puppet a whole body, you can join more bags to the body bag—two for short legs and four for longer legs with joints. If you wish, you can make the body with just a flat sheet of paper. See Illus. 255. The body will then dangle lightly as you move the head about. Try making both kinds of bodies to see the different effects.

Illus. 257. This creature's pipe-cleaner antennae have been covered with tinfoil. He has black button eyes.

Illus. 258. One of the creations in Illus. 256 is now a finished product.

demonstrates, the upper lip of the mouth is drawn on the lower edge of the flap, and the lower lip is drawn on the body of the bag—a little beneath the flap. Now when the flap goes up and down, the figure will seem to be talking. Which way you make the head will depend on whether you want your figure to be expressive with its eyes or mouth —a combination of both will help give variety in a cast of characters.

Illus. 259. Despite his pink cheeks and gay orange and red polka dots, this little clown-like figure has an unhappy look. Notice how fancy his costume is because of the ruffles under his chin and on top of his head. A green pointed cap with a pompon completes his outfit.

Illus. 260. Large paper drinking cups give this strange character very protruding eyes. Wallpaper decorates his body and crepe-paper bow tie, and forms his long legs. It even makes a row of protruding teeth! With a flower to decorate his hat, he looks ready to take on the world.

Illus. 261. Have you ever seen a purple cat? Bottle tops make perfect shiny eyes, and its whiskers are made of straw. Its handsome companion has ears lined with cotton batting, and straggling yarn hair. His eyes alternate colors, and his nose has the same colors as his eyes.

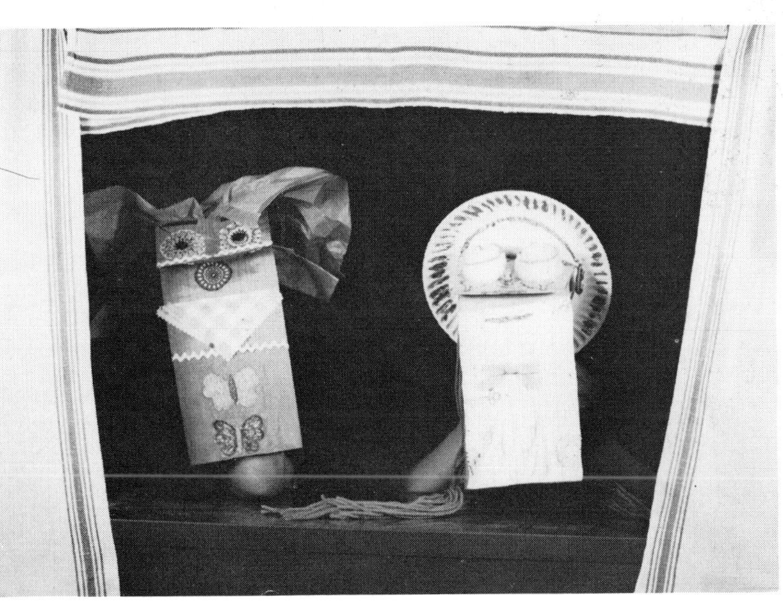

Illus. 262. Two strange characters are having a dialogue on the stage which has been constructed. Note the fancy eyes, butterflies and flowing hair which decorate the character on the left, and the paper pie-plate hat on his partner.

Illus. 263. Fish swim gently in the air, suspended by two wires in the form of an X. Each wire moves independently of the other. The crepe-paper strips were moved along the wire until the entire mobile was in balance. The shapes were made by stretching tissue paper across thin wire frames.

13. Making Mobiles

Mobiles, a form of sculpture invented by Alexander Calder, are composed of hanging objects which are ideally balanced in such a way that every part of the construction moves. The one in Illus. 263, for example, consists of colored shapes attached with strips of crepe paper to two pieces of wire, which are in turn hanging from a pipe cleaner.

It is much easier to make a mobile while it is hanging, in order to balance it. You can also see it as a whole while you are working on it and make substitutions and additions more easily. Wire, clothesline or heavy string can be attached to some kind of support, and you can connect string, wire or thread to it—whatever you want to suspend your objects on.

If you want to make a mobile entirely out of

Illus. 264.

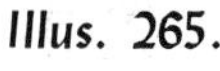

Illus. 265.

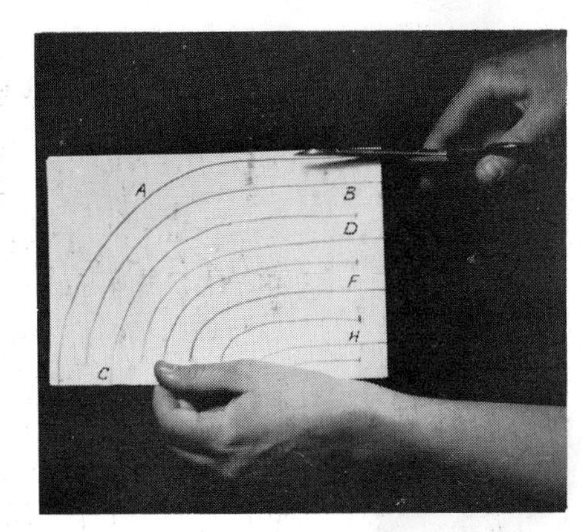

Illus. 266.

paper, you can explore the different ways to fold and cut the paper sheet so that it will result in a mobile. Some of these ways are demonstrated to start you off.

First, fold a sheet of paper lengthwise, as shown in Illus. 264. Fold it again in the opposite direction, so that you have a rectangle with two folded sides and two non-folded (Illus. 265). Then round the corner of the two non-folded sides (Line A in Illus. 266). Cut a slit, beginning from one folded side and ending about ½ inch from the opposite side (Line B in Illus. 267).

Start now from the side at which you just ended (Line C in Illus. 267) and continue to alternate your slits. When all the slits have been made and you unfold your paper completely, it should resemble the oval shape in Illus. 268.

Now, holding the unfolded oval in the exact middle, shake it so that the strips will fall below. See if your mobile looks like the one in Illus. 269. Several of these, cut from paper of varying colors and sizes, could be hung by threads to a wire in order to make a large mobile.

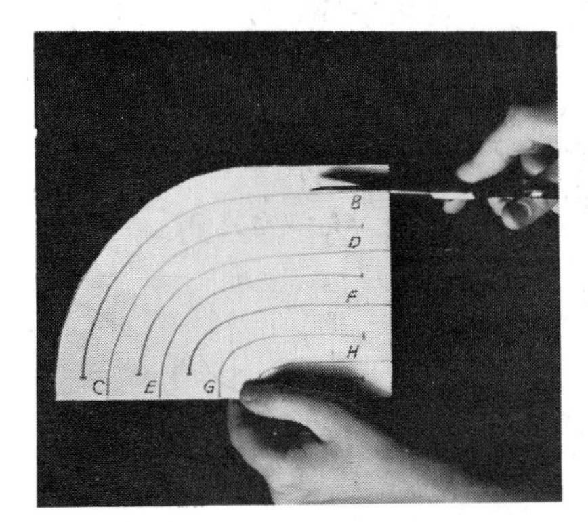

Illus. 267.

Illus. 268.

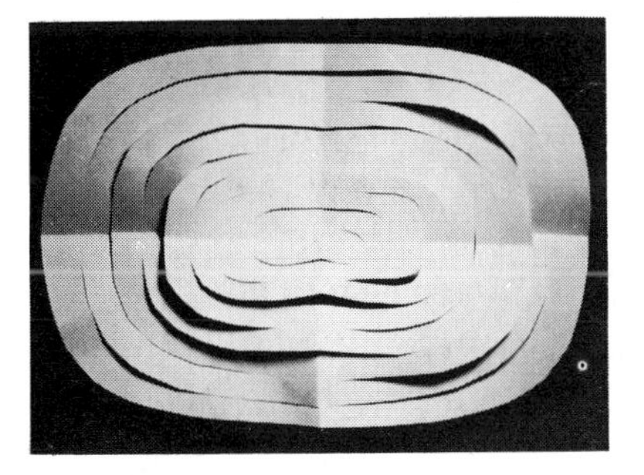

Illus. 269.

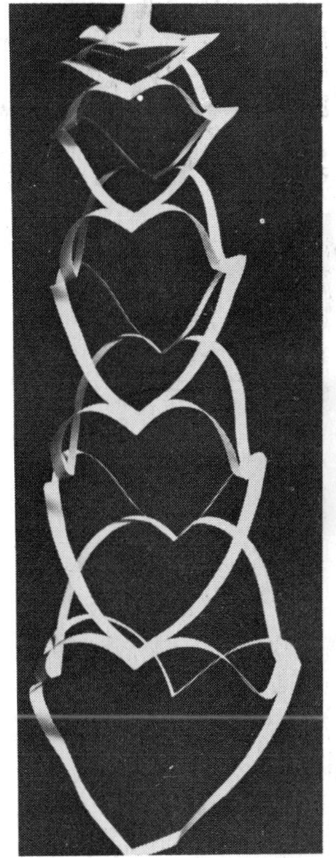

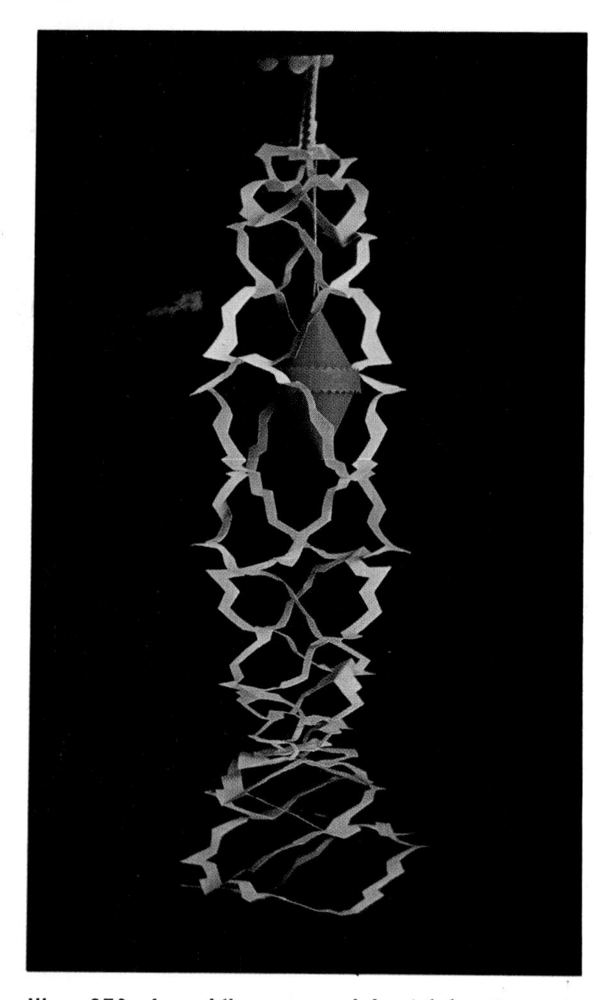

Illus. 270. A mobile composed by joining two sets of zigzag strips together, end-to-end. Within it is suspended a bright orange top. It is truly hanging by a thread! The orange top is made by glueing two construction-paper cones together.

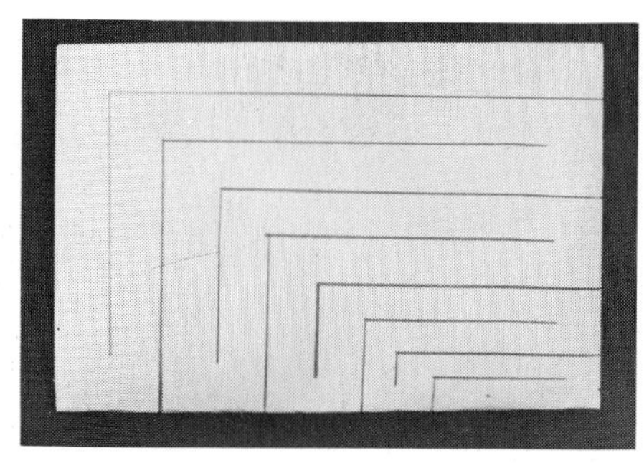

Illus. 271. Straight, right-angled lines cut in the folded rectangle form the mobile shown in Illus. 272.

Illus. 272. A wide paper mobile, cut with angular slits rather than curved.

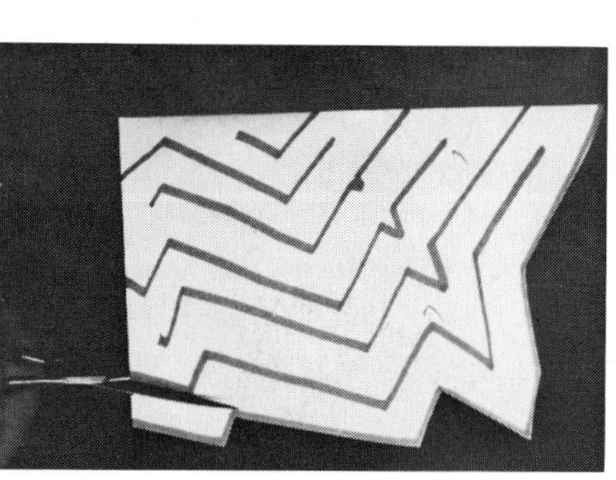

Illus. 273. Zigzag or jagged slits in the folded rectangle produced the mobile in Illus. 270 (Left). Experiment yourself with the kind of slits which can be cut.

Illus. 274.

Illus. 275.

To make the more closely woven mobile in Illus. 276, you can cut slits in a thrice-folded sheet of paper. Fold your paper twice into a rectangle, as you have been doing for the first few paper mobiles. Turn the rectangle so that the corner between the *folded* sides is the lower right-hand corner.

Now bring the upper right-hand corner across to the lower folded edge, making a diagonal fold across the rectangle (Illus. 274). Trim the base of the now-formed triangle, as indicated by the black line in Illus. 274. Cut alternating slits across the triangle, as you did to make the former mobiles (Illus. 275).

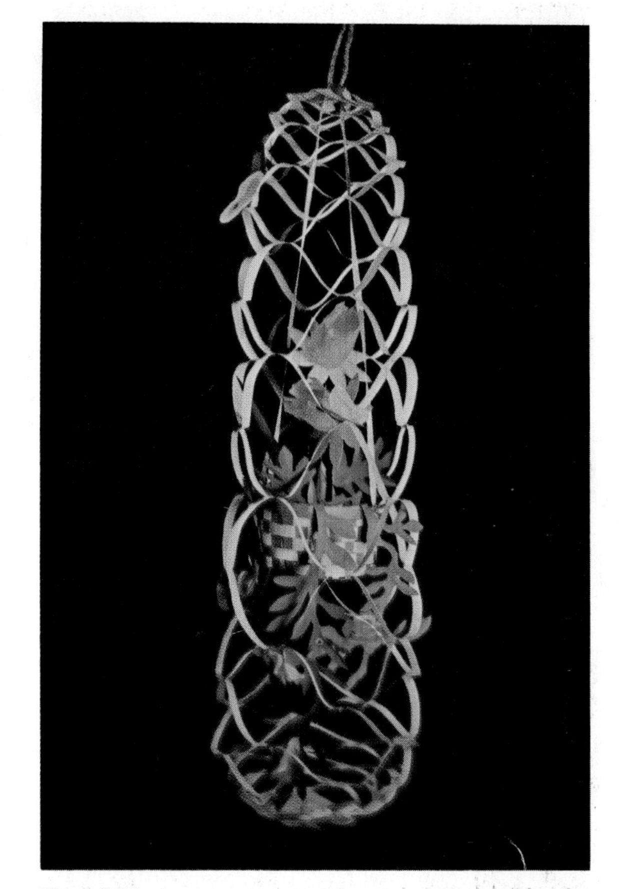

Illus. 276. Leaves seem to be growing outside the mobile, and a pink butterfly has stopped to rest upon a curve.

The one in Illus. 276 was made by cutting two paper mobiles with this technique and then combining them end-to-end. It encloses a basket of yellow daffodils, suspended by two ribbons from the same pipe cleaner from which the mobile hangs. The basket has been woven with paper strips; the leaves and petals cut out of construction paper. The budlike petals were formed with tissue paper (see Chapter 10 for information on flowers).

Illus. 277. Two mobiles of orange flint paper were joined end-to-end and then filled with crushed orange cellophane paper to make this ornate mobile. A horizontal ring of pipe cleaners, covered with orange tissue paper encircles the mobile at its middle. The ring has been hung by means of shiny yellow ribbon to the top of the mobile. Stars and strands of curled yellow ribbon hang from the ring, as well as small vertical strands of orange tissue paper.

Illus. 278. Three strings hold objects of different shapes and sizes. Each shape will move independently of the others. You may want to experiment with this kind of mobile first to see the variety of shapes you can make.

Illus. 279.

14. Slit and Slide Technique

You can make three-dimensional objects with flat sheets of paper rather than folded or curled sheets if you use the "slit and slide" technique. This consists of cutting slits into two flat shapes and sliding them together perpendicular to each other. The figures shown in the two illustrations are a bit difficult to begin with, so try the cat shown on page 144 before you do these.

Illus. 279 shows the parts of an animal before it is put together with the slit and slide technique. The parts are all made of corrugated cardboard. In order to make each part symmetrical, the pattern for each one was cut out of folded newspaper, then traced on to the corrugated cardboard. The only exception to this was the animal's body. Its design was placed directly on the cardboard. All parts were then painted with black and blue tempera paint.

The small, modernistic animal in Illus. 280 has been made with construction paper. Its legs and wings were cut from folded paper to make them symmetrical. Slits were cut in the wings and the blue paper feathers, then slid together. A long, curly tail was pasted to the rear section of its body. The animal's head has been made in an interesting manner, giving the creation a touch of modern art. Concentric, diminishing circles were placed each within the other and fitted together by small slits.

The simple cat, seen in Illus. 281–3, shows more clearly the steps of the slit and slide technique.

Illus. 280.

Illus. 281.

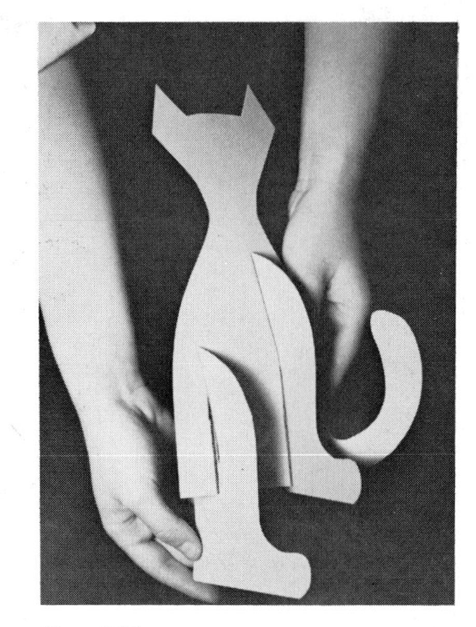

Illus. 282.

Illus. 283.

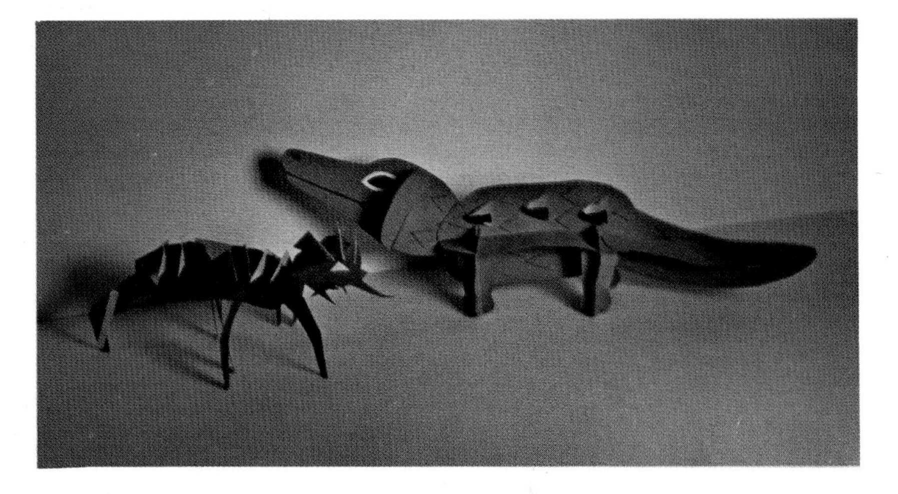

Illus. 284. Two interesting animals stop for a friendly chat before passing on their way. Whether solidly built, such as the green smiling chap on the right, or delicately moulded, like the one on the left who is inching its way along, these three-dimensional animals will be fun to construct.

In Illus. 281 are the parts of the cat before it is put together. Two vertical slits are cut into the body, beginning from its lower edge. Each of the two legs has also been cut with a vertical slit, starting from the *top* edge. Illus. 282 shows how the legs are fitted to the body—they are slid in perpendicular to it. In Illus. 283 is the standing cat, looking quite happy with its accomplishment!

In Illus. 284 are two animals which are a bit more complicated than the cat. Their bodies were constructed first, and then the horizontal ears, legs, and feathers were cut out of folded construction paper and placed exactly halfway across the vertical bodies. Small V-shapes were cut in the body, tail and head of the animal on the right, and some were bent slightly outward.

See what you can do now to represent the animal world with the use of this technique. Experiment with legs, wings, heads and tails to see what shapes you can come up with. Cardboard and tagboard, as well as paper can be used. Whether imaginary or real, the animals will form an interesting menagerie.

The slit and slide technique can also be used to put three-dimensional abstract designs together. In Illus. 285 a colorful, symmetrical one has been constructed completely from construction paper. The red strips which form the base were attached together first. Small crowns were also slid into the corners where the red strips interlock.

Two large, half-moon shapes are placed diagonally across the rectangular base, and they in turn support a large green octagonal shape. The yellow crowns which decorate its surface echo the motif of the crowns perched on the base. Four interlocking green and yellow circles are then fitted to the green hexagon, to give another repeating design.

Illus. 285. An abstract design made with the slit and slide technique. More shapes can still be added to these to make a larger design. Experiment yourself with abstracts as well as representational designs.

Illus. 286. A ghostly tree seems to rise up out of the night. Two tree shapes were made out of tagboard and then fitted together. Pipe cleaners were attached to the trunk and branches for support and color. Leaves, cut from paper, were also interlocked together for the three-dimensional effect, and then fitted to the branches of the tree.

Illus. 287. Potted flowers are cleverly constructed by the slit and slide technique. The pot is composed of two pieces of tagboard, making a sturdy support for the flowers. The blossoms are made of interlocked paper. Pipe cleaners are attached behind green stems for support.

Illus. 288. This paper pillow denizen of the deep is $2\frac{1}{2}$ x 2 feet in size. His harmonious color pattern was created with tempera paints with some green, gold and silver Christmas glitter added to provide highlights.

15. Paper Pillow Figures

Paper pillow figures allow still another method for making three-dimensional figures. Now you will be able to make a really plump Thanksgiving turkey, a substantial Santa Claus, or a sleek fat cat—because you will stuff them with paper just the way a pillow is stuffed with down.

To begin, place six unfolded sheets of newspaper on top of one another. Using pencil, crayon, chalk or paint, draw an outline of your figure on the top sheet. Try to make the figure almost as large as the newspaper (Illus. 289). Since you will undoubtedly find it difficult to cut through six sheets at once, cut through the top three first. Then, using your top cut-out shape as a guide, cut the three remaining sheets. Now pile all six together again.

You are ready to "sew" your sheets together. The dotted lines in Illus. 290 indicate where you will, with a staple, sew the papers together. However, you can if you prefer paste little paper strips around the papers so that they lap over on the two sides and the edge of the pillow as in Illus. 291. Keep these strips rather small and narrow if possible.

When you have approximately three-fourths of the figure sewn up, start stuffing. Bathroom tissue, facial tissue, napkins, crushed newspaper, or even foam rubber are fine stuffing materials. Be sure to stuff the thinnest parts of the figure first, such as tails, arms, legs, etc. It is important when first planning your figure, that its parts are not too narrow to allow for stuffing.

Decorating your pillow comes next. Although you will probably want to paint all or part of the figures, there are many other means of decoration at your fingertips.

Scrap materials can easily be applied. A human figure can be adorned with hair made of yarn, string, unravelled binder twine, cotton batting, drinking straws, broom straws, etc. Jewelry can be added

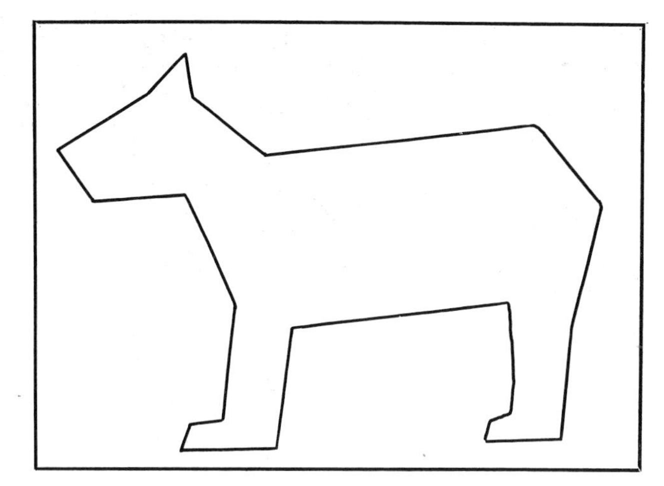

Illus. 289. Step I in making a pillow figure.

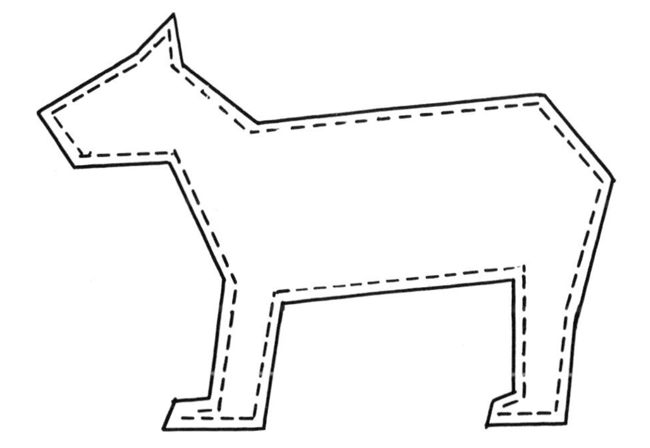

Illus. 290. The sheets of paper can be "sewn" with staples along these dotted lines.

Illus. 291. Or you can glue strips of paper over the layers of newspaper to hold the figure together.

Illus. 292. A mischievous wink characterizes a paper pillow cat. Made from a large circle of papers, he has construction-paper eyelashes, broom-bristle whiskers and painted fur patterns.

in the form of real earrings, bracelets, buttons, brooches.

Old pieces of clothing can be fashioned into stockings, trousers, shirts, skirts, hats.

Textured surfaces are available in the form of glued-on macaroni, beads, dry cereal, buttons, sequins, rice, split peas, watermelon seeds, colored popcorn, pebbles, sea shells. For these materials, Elmer's glue or Duco cement are good adhesives. If you want, you can paint over some of the harder materials with tempera. Such grainy things as rice, barley and oats tend to flake, but a coat of shellac, clear varnish or lacquer will hold the pieces in place and add a nice gloss, too.

Rice and popcorn take to soaking in food coloring very well. Try soaking some of the other materials in watercolors or dyes to see how they are affected.

A glittering surface for fish or turtles is provided by crushed glass marbles. If you cannot find ready-crushed ones, do it yourself by placing them in a pan of hot water on the stove and boiling vigorously. Scoop them out quickly and drop into ice-cold water. The marbles will shatter.

Three-dimensional protrusions of all kinds can be made in the surface of a pillow. An X shape, such as that in Illus. 293, can be repeated all over the figure. By making incisions in the form of the X through the top sheet of newspaper and pulling the tabs back as in Illus. 294, you can paint the underlying layer in a contrasting color to the folded-back tabs, making an interesting pattern.

Arch-shaped incisions, such as in Illus. 295, can be folded along the dotted line indicated and result in finlike protrusions, or you might make a furlike effect by following the pattern in Illus. 296. Here a number of parallel slits cut into a finlike protrusion can be folded forward and curled or twisted any which way.

Another colorful turtle is shown in Illus. 298. This busy swimmer was painted all over with orange tempera, and black tempera lines formed the typical shell divisions. Then circular tissue-paper shapes were placed within the divisions and spattered with

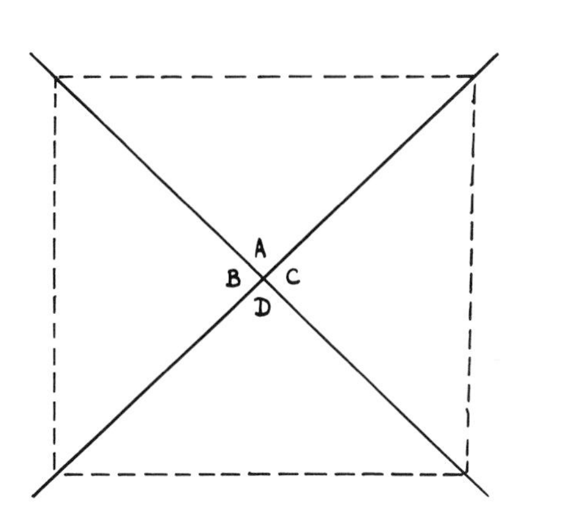

Illus. 293. To make an unusual three-dimensional pattern, draw X shapes all over your pillow. Cut along the solid lines carefully.

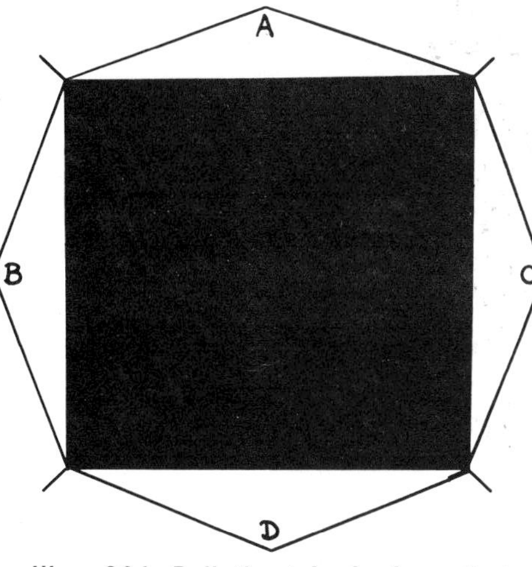

Illus. 294. Pull the tabs back so that you have a window like this. Paint the underlying layer in a contrasting color.

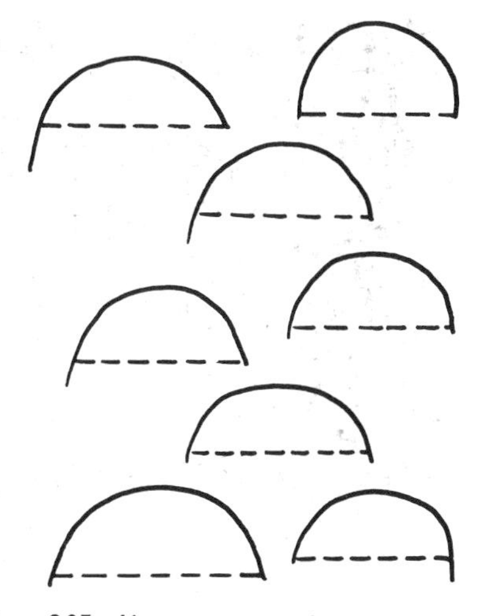

Illus. 295. If you are making a fish, you could make finlike three-dimensional protrusions by following this pattern.

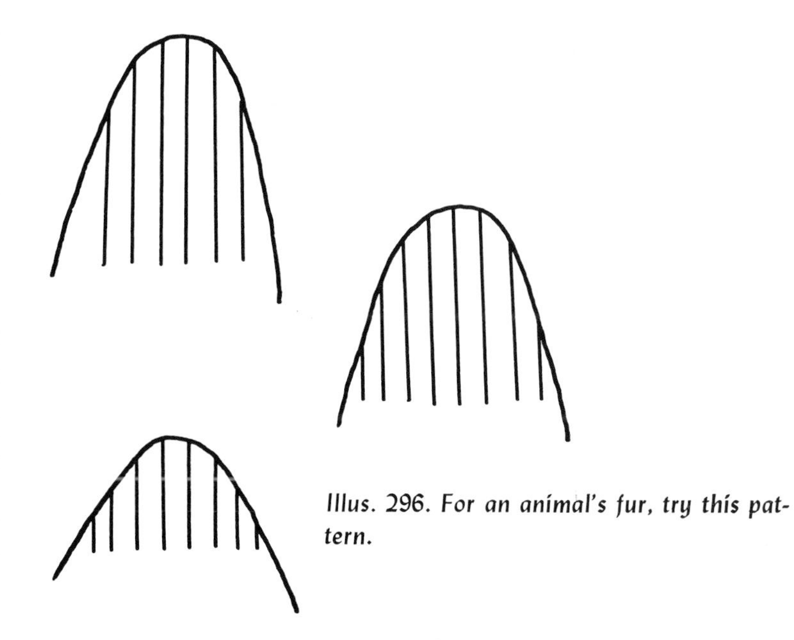

Illus. 296. For an animal's fur, try this pattern.

Illus. 297. This pillow fish was made from layers of rice paper. A fine brush and watercolors were used to decorate him. The many different patterns—crosses, solids, checkerboards, and dabs make him look like a patchwork quilt.

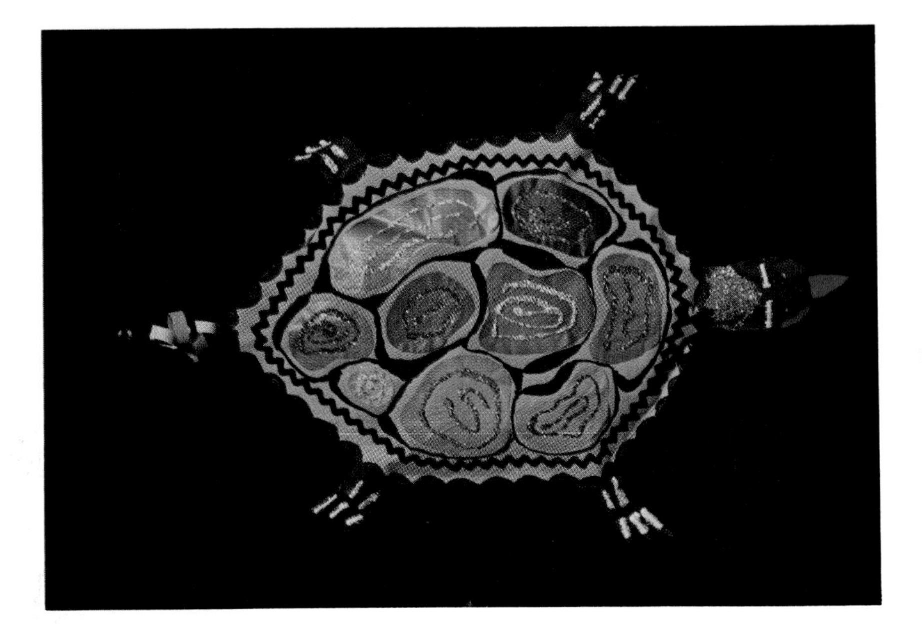

Illus. 298. A richly colored turtle pillow, decorated with temperas, glitter, rick-rack, and tissue paper.

Illus. 299. Here is a three-dimensional protrusion that you can curl round a pencil.

Christmas glitter mixed with glue. A black rick-rack border outlines the shell and its scalloped pattern is repeated with a black tempera design along the outermost edge of the shell. Strips of construction paper were curled and glued in place for a realistic turtle tail. A red construction-paper tongue and glitter eyes complete the figure.

The fanciful red fish paper pillow in Illus. 300 displays a number of shapes and designs. He has been painted with subtly varying shades of red, and, in the mid-section, with light strokes of white. Scalloped white paint lines and black blobs suggest fish scales. Pieces of a white paper doily make a fancy tail fin and head trim. White rick-rack defines his dorsal and ventral fins.

The little green tufts on his tail and nose were made from strands of yarn which were wound round a hand and tied in the middle with a piece of yarn.

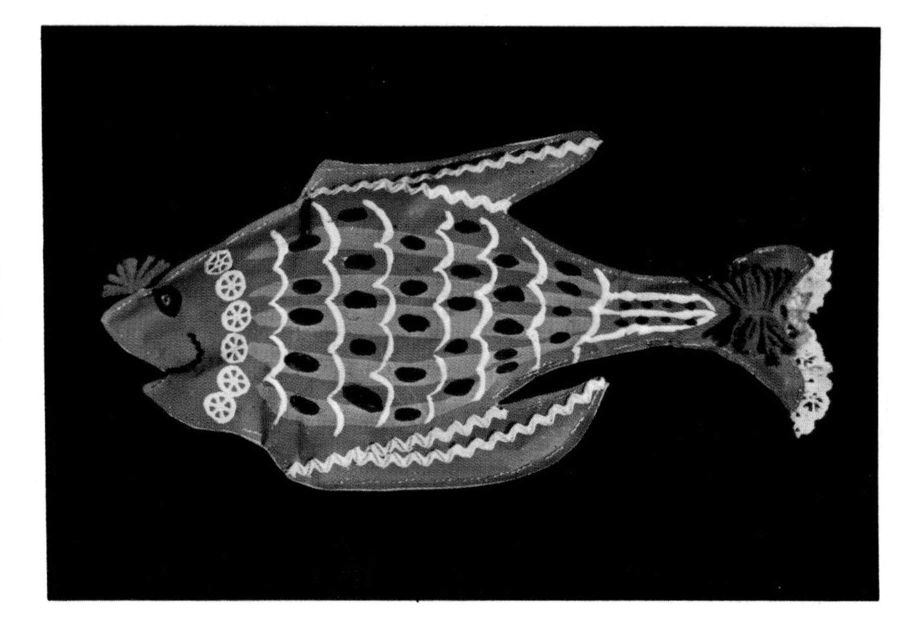

Illus. 300. Another fancy sea dweller—a red fish. Yarn, rick-rack, paper doilies, and tempera paints make a very decorative paper pillow.

The looped portions were cut to make a fringe effect.

You might make a three-dimensional fin pattern such as is shown in Illus. 301.

Another means of decorating paper pillow figures is with crayons. Since you are using newspaper for your figures, you might place the classified-ad section on top and use the columns to make a geometric pattern. In crayon decorating, you will need a hard surface to work on. Therefore, it is advisable to make your design before you sew and stuff. Illus. 302 shows such a design.

If you should choose to make a crayon-resist design you might better use light-colored crayons which will resist the black tempera paint you apply over them.

It is not, of course, necessary that you use

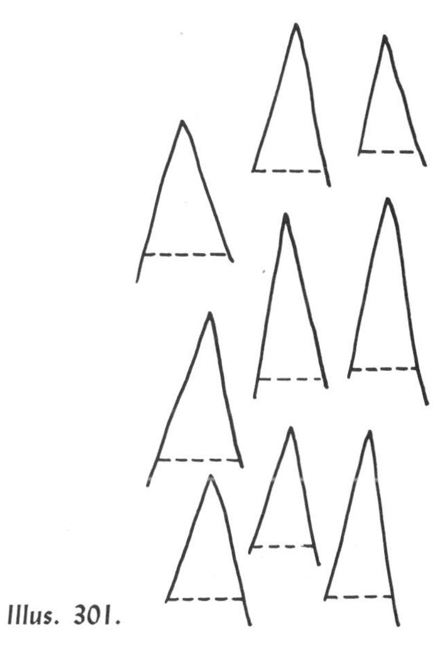

Illus. 301.

Illus. 302. A geometric crayon design, made on the classified-ad section of the newspaper, can be used as the top layer of your paper pillow.

newspaper for the outer layer of your pillow. You could even use a piece of cloth.

Paper pillow people are great fun to make, since it is possible to make a life-size replica of yourself, someone you know, or a character from fiction.

If you want to make a self-portrait, use long brown wrapping paper instead of newspaper. Lie down on the top sheet and have someone draw your silhouette around you.

When making human figures it is a good idea to observe the body parts in action since you will want to make a figure running, sitting, kneeling, or even dancing.

A number of paper pillows can be assembled to make one large figure. You might have one big body pillow, a head pillow, and three pillows each for the arms and legs (Illus. 303). The pillow parts can be joined by brass paper fasteners.

A large paper-pillow person can be decorated with real clothing, a synthetic wig and marble eyes. A small pillow figure might wear doll's clothing, or you could paint, crayon, or chalk on the features and garments.

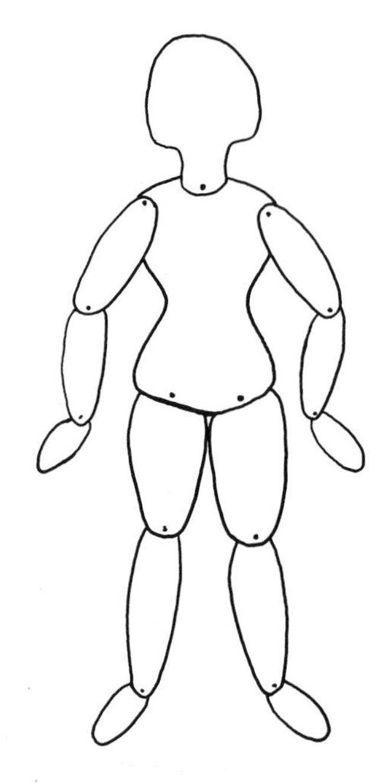

Illus. 303. A very large paper-pillow person can be made from many small pillows. This figure's pillow parts are held together by brass paper fasteners which serve as hinges so that the arms, legs and head can be moved to assume a variety of poses.

16. The Diorama

You can get further pleasure with your paper-sculptured figures by creating a three-dimensional diorama with them. A diorama is a painting seen through an opening—by placing your figures within something you will be making a theatrical scene upon a stage. You can make up your own scenes, or use familiar ones from plays and stories. A dramatic moment from a fairy tale might inspire you, for example, or a lovely setting from a movie, opera or operetta.

To begin your diorama, carefully select the cardboard box in which you will place the figures. The size of your box will be important, because you want to have the correct size ratio between your figures and the objects which will surround them—trees, houses, mountains, etc.—as well as the ratio of all the objects to the surrounding enclosure. Therefore, if your box is small your figures will have to be very tiny, and they'll be harder to construct and see. If your box is an enormous one, your paper objects will be large also, and will have to be reinforced with cardboard to stand up. A box which is just a few inches larger than a shoebox should provide a good, medium-sized stage.

Illus. 304. Angora yarn covers the kittens searching for missing mittens. Real fall leaves decorate the stage, and a cylinder wishing well is on the far right.

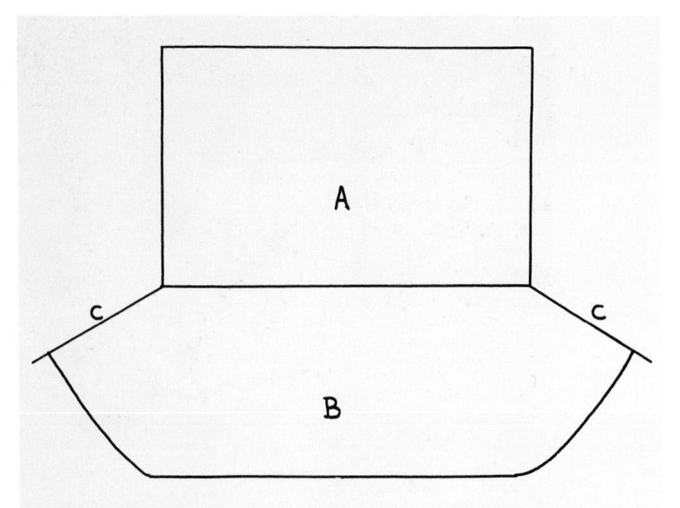

Illus. 306. A piece of cardboard cut in this shape can be added to the stage to make an extra floor piece. Section A is placed over the regular floor; section B forms the new front. The side flaps can be taped to the extra piece at line C.

Place your box on a side, so that its bottom will serve as the back of the stage. In order to make sure there is enough lighting on the stage, you can cut out the side which forms the ceiling. If you want the stage to have a top, however, to hang such things as a chandelier or tree foliage, you can cut a rectangle in the ceiling near the back.

A backdrop, also made of cardboard, can be added to your stage. This will decrease the size of your stage area. By making two vertical folds in the backdrop, you can have diagonal walls between the back and sides of the stage. This will enable anyone to see the whole stage from the extreme right or left—diagonal walls are in a legitimate theatre for this purpose. When making the vertical folds, measure the backdrop against the back of the box and score the lines (see page 56) so that you can place the folds exactly. Your backdrop can also be a semicircular one—tagboard is a good material to use in this case.

By placing the backdrop a few inches in front of the back of the box, you will have the opportunity to create an illusion of great depth. You can, for example, cut windows and doors in your backdrop, and paint mountains or meadows and rolling hills on the inside of the extreme back of the stage. The viewer's eye will then be drawn through the openings in the backdrop to the distant scenery behind it, and the effect will be that of a great deal of space. The windows can be covered with cellophane, to give them a realistic touch. To throw light on the distant scene, cut a rectangle out of the ceiling between the backdrop and back. If you want light on your backdrop also, you can cut a rectangle in front of this as well. Experiment yourself with different lighting techniques. Perhaps you could get a bulb into a lower corner of the stage, or a whole row of them across the front of the stage as footlights. If you do have footlights, you might want to put a strip of cardboard across the opening to cover them.

If you keep the flaps of the carton on it, you can bend the top flap upward and use it to announce the subject of your theme. Either draw right on the flap with crayon or tempera, or paste on letters cut out from paper. By bringing all four flaps forward so that each one extends a side, you can of course increase the depth of the stage. Or you can just increase the floor by cutting off the upper flap and bending the two side flaps outward, as is shown in Illus. 307.

You might wish to create a floor section out

of cardboard which will extend even farther out towards the audience, and also will reach sideways to the flaps when they are bent diagonally outward. You can then tape the sides to the extra piece. Illus. 306 shows the floor section before it is added to the stage.

Curtains can be added to give a touch of authenticity. Cloth or crepe paper can be attached to florist's wire, baling wire or pipe cleaners which run across the top front of the stage. Fold the top inch of the cloth or crepe paper over the wire and hem it with straight pins, thread or glue. The wire or pipe cleaners can be inserted through holes in the upper two front corners of the box, and knotted on the outside so it will stay. Illus. 310 shows a stage with a curtain.

After you get your stage assembled you will be ready to add the figures, buildings and scenery. The three-dimensional figures and objects can be monofold forms, as described in Chapter 5. Cone figures (Chapter 7) or cylindrical ones (Chapter 8) can be employed. Or the slit and slide technique described in Chapter 14 might be used to make the characters of your drama and their setting. You could combine techniques, having both round figures and flat ones on-stage.

In Illus. 307, a line from a popular round is being portrayed. A woman is about to cut off the tails of three sightless mice. Trees crayoned on construction paper make up the background, as well as a tagboard tree made with the slit and slide technique. Cotton batting has been dabbed with green paint to suggest its leaves, and pipe cleaners behind the tree give it support. The woman and the mice are paper-cone constructions, with arms and legs made of pipe cleaners.

In Illus. 308 are Mary and her tag-along friend,

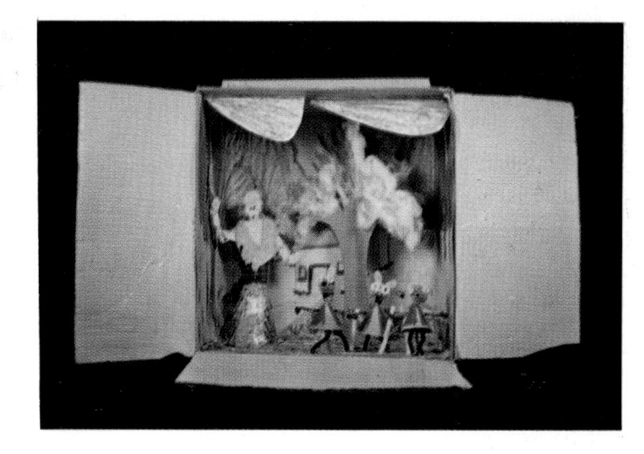

Illus. 307. The floor of the diorama in this scene displays a walk made of wrinkled tissue paper which has been covered with glue and sand. The lady's fancy skirt is made out of tinfoil which covers chocolate Easter eggs, and her shawl is made from an old towel.

both made of tagboard and constructed with the slit and slide technique. The flat, two-dimensional figures have been painted with tempera.

Illus. 309 portrays several people surrounding a mulberry bush as they act out the different verses of the song. By putting the box within its cover, the floor space of the stage is enlarged.

You may recognize the tale that is being portrayed in Illus. 310. In case you don't, it is a scene from "The Pied Piper of Hamlin." The sense of depth in this stage is shown in many ways. The bottom flap is extended forward, a backdrop of paper has had buildings painted on it, and a paper picket fence has been placed a few inches in front of the backdrop. The construction-paper house also has depth with its open windows, door, and green paper steps. Brown construction paper covers the floor, with cobblestones of black crayon drawn on it. In the foreground, the figure on the left is

Illus. 308. Pipe cleaners support a pretty girl and her lamb. The background is chiefly a painted one, the red roofs balanced with a red ribbon on the lamb and the red on Mary's dress. Notice how the sky curves to the front of the box.

Illus. 309. These smiling people are cone figures from the waist down and two-dimensional paper from the waist up. The trunk and branches of the mulberry bush are made with pipe cleaners and paper—the mountains are painted on the backs and sides of the box.

Illus. 310. Green velvet curtains attached to pipe cleaners give this diorama a theatrical touch.

dressed in cloth while the one on the right is clothed chiefly in tissue paper. You can see that either cloth or tissue paper will do nicely for costumes. Both of these figures are cone-shaped with pipe-cleaner arms. Materials that were used to decorate them include nylon stockings, corduroy, cotton balls, toothpicks, embroidery floss, human hair, pearls and velveteen. In the background at the extreme left is a monofold little girl who is leaning against the fence in front of a monofold tree.

Illus. 311 is a scene from the days of King Arthur. Materials rich in color and texture are used to decorate the castle scene. Green velvet, trimmed with gold ribbon, makes the tapestry on the wall and the contrasting background to the red throne. The throne itself is a complex structure—the high back is made of tagboard covered with red tissue paper. Its lower half is composed of a thread spool surrounded by red rug filler. Construction paper covered with a light watercolor wash and pencil outline suggests the stone wall in back.

The fair damsel has a cone body, her knight-errant a cylinder one. Both have small cotton balls for heads with hair of unravelled binder twine.

Illus. 311. The knight who is kneeling to his lady is wearing a green cloth garment trimmed with Christmas glitter, which also trims the lady's dress. Note the stained glass window which is cut in the right side of the stage.

In Illus. 312, Cinderella is being put upon the stage. Her helpful fairy godmother is in the background—a two-dimensional figure cut out of white construction paper and suspended from the ceiling by a pipe cleaner. Cinderella has a pipe-cleaner body, and is clothed in paper towelling. Her head is made of a ball of tissue paper which has been covered with starch-soaked strips of tissue.

The background of Illus. 313 is a circular one of white paper, washed with transparent watercolor to suggest the ocean. Aquarium gravel, shells and stones are glued to the floor of the diorama, and a mesh vegetable bag hangs over the front left side to suggest a fisherman's net. If the fisherman wishes to use it he could catch many colorful two-dimensional fish, each supported by a pipe cleaner which has been poked into the floor.

Illus. 312. Real grasses and weeds are used in the background of this familiar fairy tale, while on the far right is a paper cylinder tree trunk topped with crumpled green tissue paper foliage.

Illus. 313. We seem to be at the bottom of a deep ocean when gazing at this diorama. Green pipe cleaners serve as seaweed, as well as bunches of crepe paper which have been split from the top.

Illus. 314. A lovely creche, its dark blue background decorated with silver stars. Paper in the form of cubes makes the supporting beams of the manger's roof and the crib. Two contrasting sheets of brown and tan paper have been cut into strips to suggest the straw on top of the roof, and slitted construction paper surrounds the crib. Joseph is a cylinder figure, while both Mary and the angel hovering above are built upon a cone shape. Tissue paper which has been folded back and forth like an Oriental fan makes the angel's wings.

Illus. 315. Rumpelstiltskin is offering his help to the miller's daughter, who must spin a large quantity of straw into gold. The background of this diorama is extremely interesting. The backdrop of painted stone has been placed a few inches in front of the real back of the stage. On the real back wall is painted the tower of a castle, a railing, and the night sky. Inside, surrounding the backdrop, painted tagboard has been shaped into long, narrow cubes to suggest heavy beams. One beam is placed directly in the middle, and it is covered with bricks cut from a magazine. Satin curtains and upper ruffle blend beautifully with the scene.

Illus. 316. Arched windows look in on the Nativity scene, and gold stars hang outside them to suggest the heavens. The ceiling of the shoebox has been replaced with a slanting roof—popsicle sticks now represent the beams. The roof is covered with construction paper and straw. Cellophane strips have been hung to give the scene a celestial touch, while the humble birth is reflected in the construction-paper cradle filled with straw. All the figures have been made from the cone shape.

Illus. 317. Betsy Ross, warm and comfortable in a cozy room, is making the first American flag. In this case it is a mixture of materials—paper stars, red felt and blue cotton strips have been placed on white satin. Betsy's body is made of pipe cleaners covered with tissue paper. A cone forms her skirt and bonnet, and cylinders make up the blouse and its sleeves. Yarn is glued in place for hair. The fireplace was made by crumpling tissue paper and pasting it against the wall, then painting bricks on it. The buffet is constructed from cardboard, while braided rag strips have been sewn together to make the rug.

Illus. 318. Cinderella is rushing downstairs after the ball. Only the first two steps are actually three-dimensional—the rest are painted on the backdrop. See Chapter 7 to find out how Cinderella acquired her skirt.

Illus. 319. Humpty Dumpty, just before his disaster. He is an empty egg shell, while the king and his men are cylindrical figures. The bow tie on our egg friend is made of a cylindrical paper holder, which has been vertically slit in the middle back so that both ends could be pulled forward. Painted plastic foam fills the bottom of the stage.

17. Tissue Paper Insect Mobiles

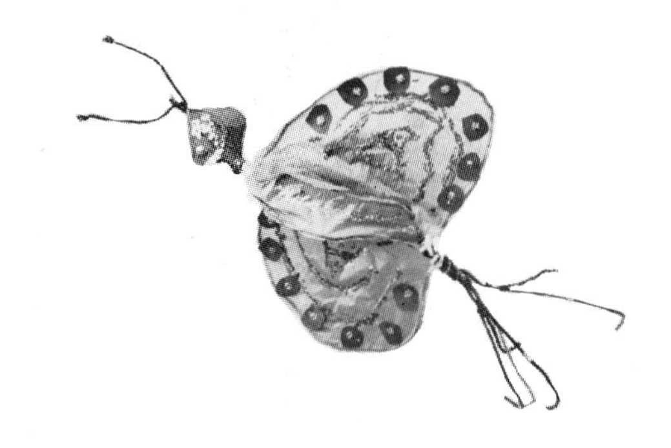

A wonderful way to combine observations of the insect world with creative work in paper is to make your own insects out of tissue paper. If you hang them as mobiles, everyone will be able to see the shapes from all directions. Try to combine the parts of insects that you have noticed—heads, eyes, legs, bodies, feelers, wings—into imaginary ones.

Illus. 320. Several insects float above the heads of the children who made them.

Illus. 321. This insect looks like a cross between a dragonfly and a ladybug. Red and yellow tissue paper cover the body frame, chartreuse tissue the wings. Green flint paper decorates the wings and forms webbed feet. Black tempera paint has been used to draw thin lines on the wings to suggest veins. This insect's unique feature is its tail, made from the plume of a hat! Single strands of the plume are also attached to the wings, and they move with the slightest breath of air.

Create your own symmetry, design, color and shape. Try exaggerating the parts of insects. Eyes can bulge, long legs can radiate from all sides of the body, many waving antennae can sprout from a head.

Consider what materials will give the insect's body contrast in color and texture. When you are finished making it, hang it by a single strand of thread—nylon will give the sturdiest support—and watch it come to life as the breeze makes it stir.

At the top of the opposite page is an insect which might be an unusual butterfly. Four pipe cleaners have been placed side by side, and then twisted together at the ends and fanned out to form a three-dimensional frame for the head. Other pipe cleaners have been placed end-to-end and twisted together to make a long body. The head and body were then twisted together.

Several pipe cleaners were joined at one end and separated to suggest a tail, and two were looped and joined to the body to form the frame for the wings. Two more were attached to the head to serve as antennae. If you make this one, make sure you have a good supply of pipe cleaners! Tissue paper was used to construct the head, body and wings. Small circles of construction paper decorate the wings, as well as Christmas glitter which has been sprinkled in circular lines.

Illus. 322. A girl begins to make the body of her insect by twisting pipe cleaners.

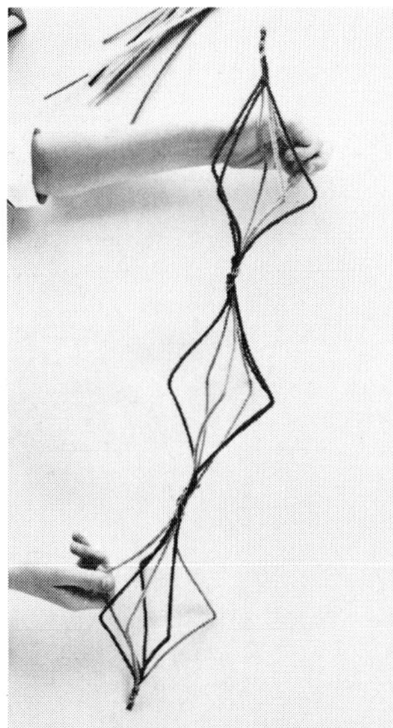

Illus. 323. Three lantern shapes are twisted together to form the body.

Illus. 324. Wings of varying sizes are added to the basic structure.

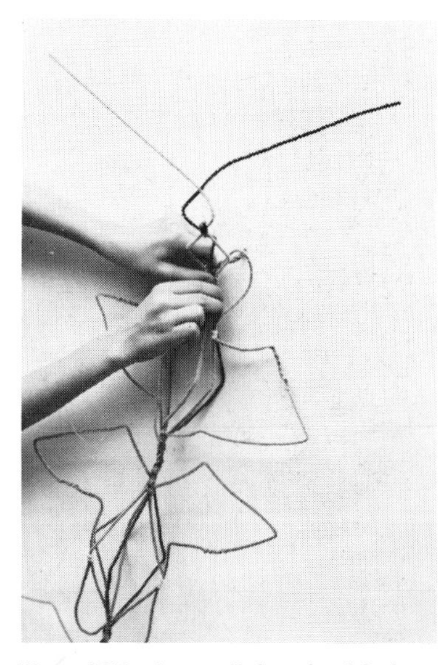

Illus. 325. A small head with long antennae is twisted on to one end.

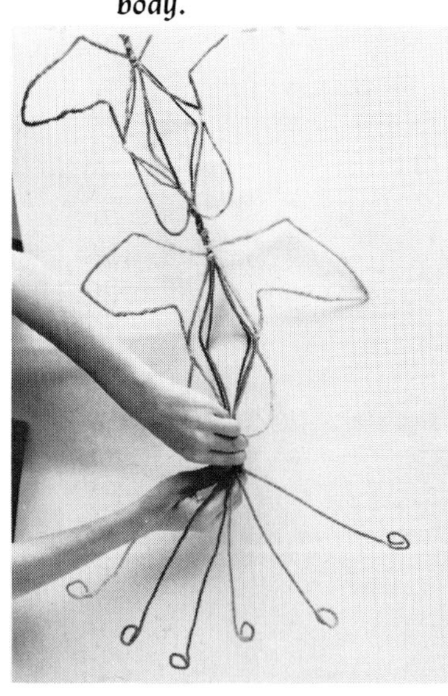

Illus. 326. The tail is added at the other end.

Illus. 327. Liquid glue is applied to a wing frame.

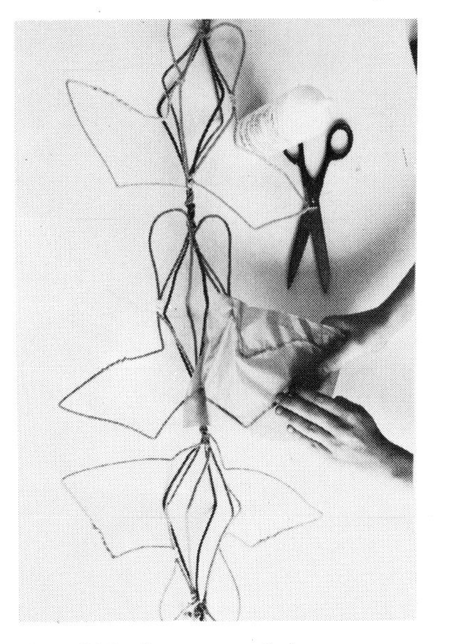

Illus. 328. A square of tissue paper is pressed upon the frame.

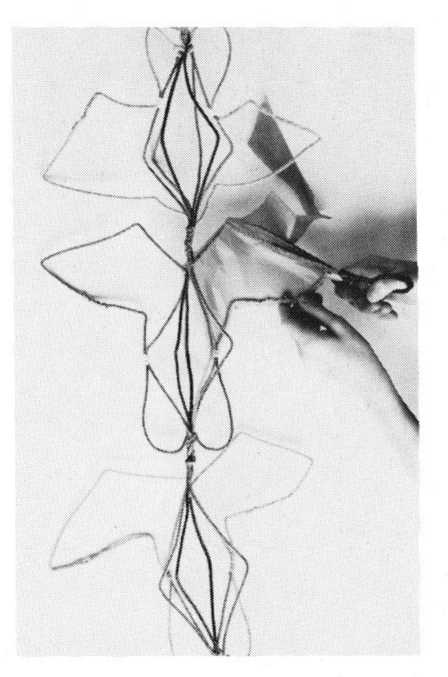

Illus. 329. The excess tissue is carefully trimmed.

Illus. 330. Parts of the frame are left uncovered to make it delicate.

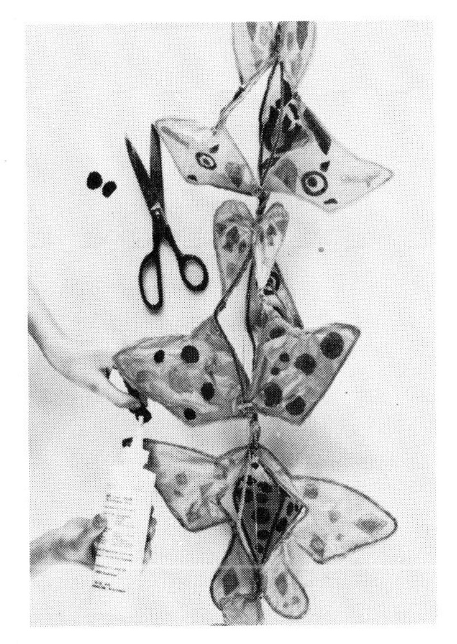

Illus. 331. Construction paper shapes are glued to the wings.

Illus. 332. Paper circles also decorate the tail for added interest.

Illus. 333. The large insect is now complete, and ready to be hung.

Illus. 334. Instead of tissue paper, plastic foam makes up the long, thin body of this insect. Yellow tissue is glued to the underneath side of each of the four wings, and clear cellophane is glued to the upper sides. Colored tissue circles are appliquéd to the cellophane. The insect's body is dotted with sequins, and two small Christmas balls attached to pipe cleaners form its protruding eyes. Dark blue foil, cut into feather shapes, make the tail of this unusual bug, and yellow rug yarn gives it a ruffled neck.

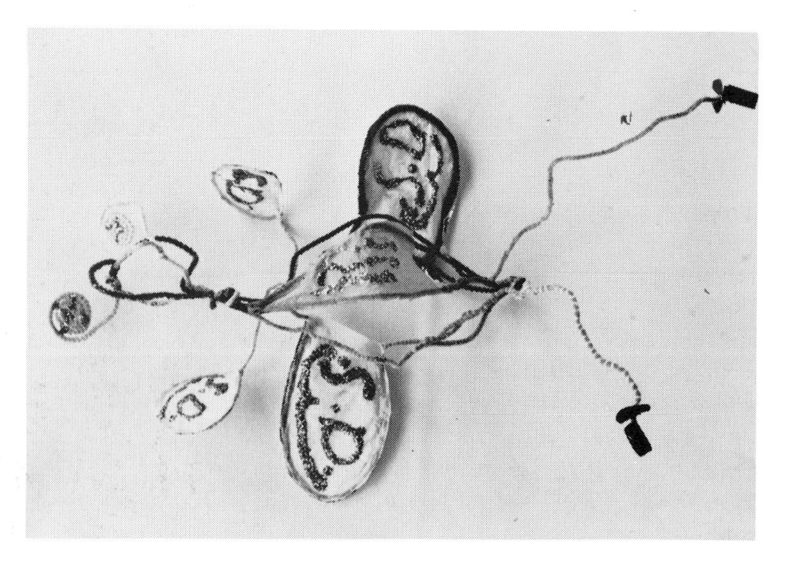

Illus. 335. The furthermost, curled pipe cleaners are the antennae of this insect. The next pair, ending in a loop, forms the creature's legs. The last two stretched-out pipe cleaners, with small paper objects attached to the ends, are its tail. The artist of this creation has left his mark by inscribing his initials with Christmas glitter on the wings and feet.

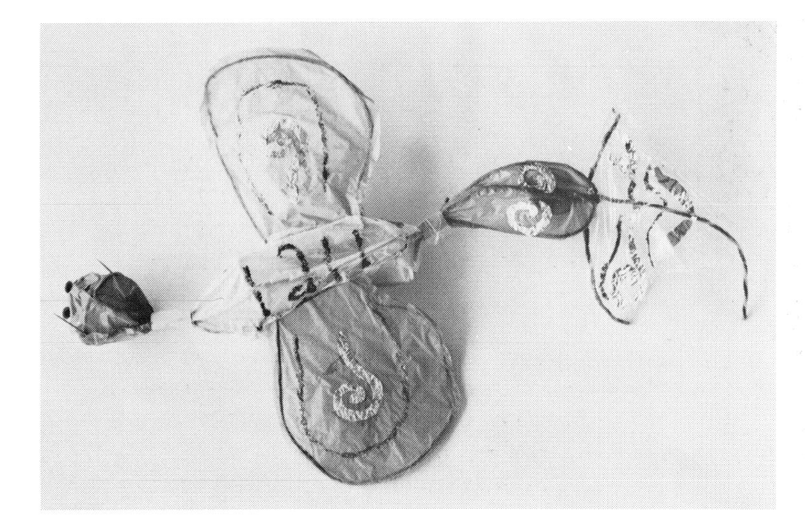

Illus. 336. A piece of baling wire supports the two-sectioned body of the insect. Two toothpicks are inserted into the head to form short antennae, and two buttons become its eyes. The tail is clear cellophane decorated with pieces of tinfoil.

Illus. 337. A lovely symmetrical, two-dimensional flying creature. Its body was made by rolling a bit of newspaper, placing it within a wire frame, and then covering the frame with green flint paper. Yellow flint paper decorates the body and wings. Two green pipe cleaners with silver beads make the antennae, and the wings are of cellophane and green flint paper. Baling wire was used to make the supporting body and the feelers which trail behind it. The feelers are covered with tinfoil and decorated with paper and tinfoil balls.

Illus. 338. One of the largest insects you'll ever see, gaily festooned with flowers. In Illus. 339 is the structure of its body frame.

Let us hope that the 4-foot-tall creature in Illus. 338 doesn't bite! Its body is composed of eight wire triangles—shown in Illus. 339—covered with purple tissue paper. Cloth daisies decorate the surface of the triangular body, tail, and green tissue wings. The head is a square wire frame covered with green and purple tissue paper. Pieces of construction paper were cut into the form of its beak, which is now open. White lace trims the edges of the beak, and shells have been placed in a circle on both sides of the box to suggest huge eyes.

Notice the little red tongue placed within the lower beak—it looks ready to say a friendly hello. Large crushed balls of tissue paper strung on two nylon threads make its gaily decorated legs, with large squares of brown construction paper forming its feet. Because the head, wings and tail had a

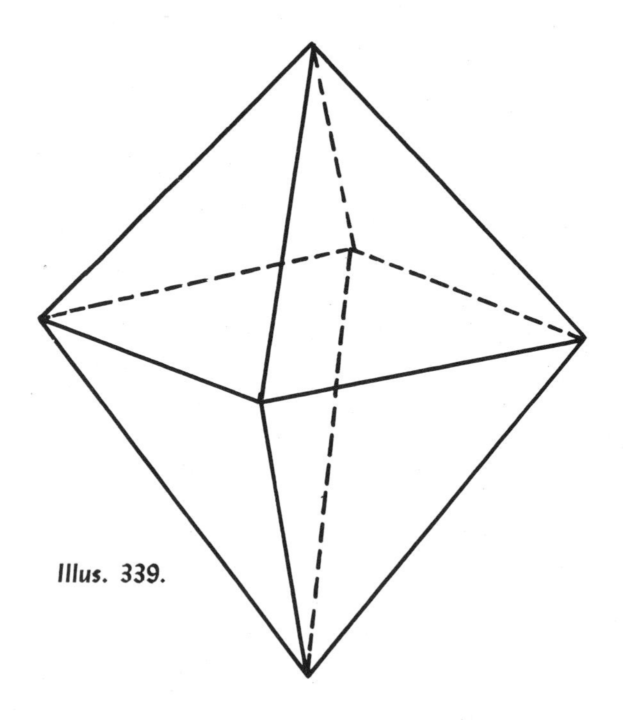

Illus. 339.

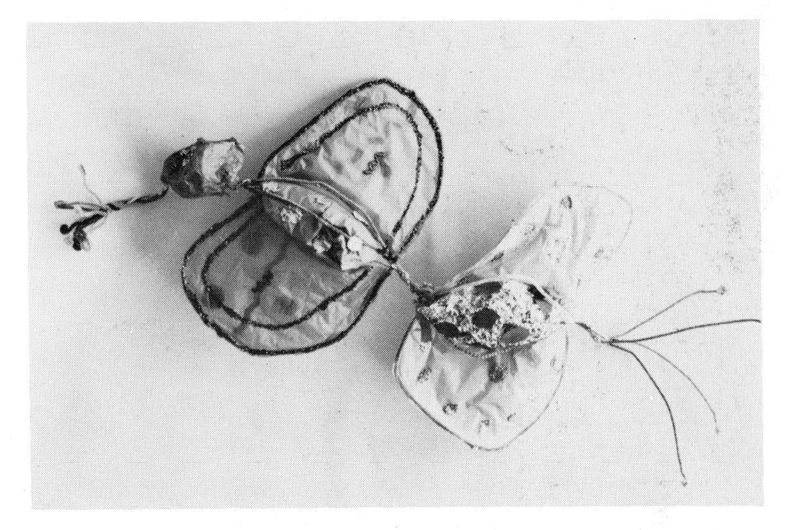

Illus. 340. A fanciful bug, having two body sections made with pipe cleaners. Instead of covering the cleaners, a tissue-covered cylinder was placed inside the pipe cleaners in the front section, and crushed tinfoil was placed inside the rear section. Baling wire runs through the insect's body for added support.

tendency to droop, they were all attached to the top of the body by means of string.

A wire frame was used instead of pipe cleaners for the figure in Illus. 338 because it was a huge one. You can use pipe cleaners as the frame to make a large insect figure, however, if you make pipe-cleaner rings for support (see Illus. 341). A series of circles, each size depending on the resultant shape of the body that you want, are placed vertically in a row. Horizontal cleaners are looped around the first circle's rim and stretched across to the next circle, looped around that, and so on, until across all of them. A number of these body shapes can be attached together to make one long body—a caterpillar, for example.

Illus. 342 demonstrates how an insect might be constructed in a very simple manner. A cylinder is used for the body, and this can be a tube from a roll of wax paper, bathroom tissue, paper towelling, or one constructed out of paper. If two holes are put in the two sides of the cylinder, wire or pipe-cleaner wing frames can be inserted. A ball of crushed tissue paper can form the head, and fanned-out pipe cleaners make a good tail.

In contrast is the rather complex insect in Illus. 340. Its body is composed of two large paper

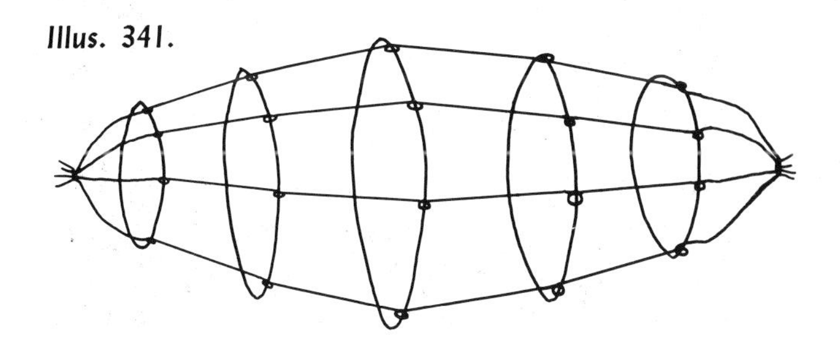

Illus. 341.

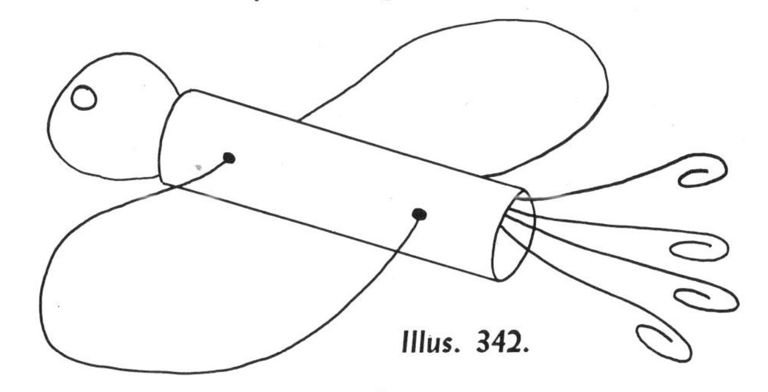

Illus. 342.

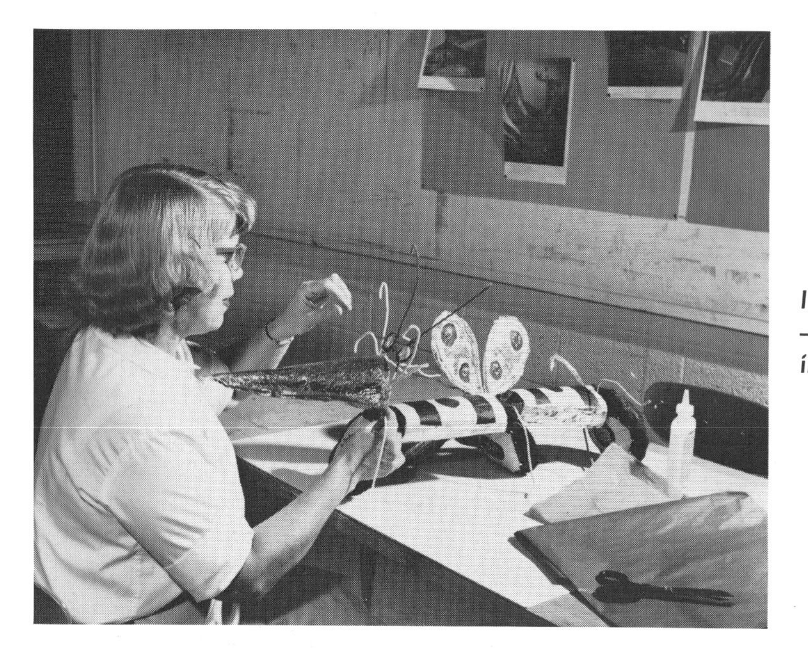

Illus. 343. An adult student at work on her paper creation —a solid, lengthy bug which seems to be patiently waiting for its finishing touches.

cylinders, stuffed with crushed tissue. A long piece of baling wire connects the head and cylinders, and the two beelike wings are made of tissue and construction paper. The legs of the bug are circular paper pillows, built around circular pieces of wire and then attached to the wire body.

Tinfoil covers the head, which is shaped like a cone, and tinfoil, construction paper and tissue paper decorate the body sections and the legs. The pipe cleaners on top of the cone head suggest eyes, whiskers and antennae.

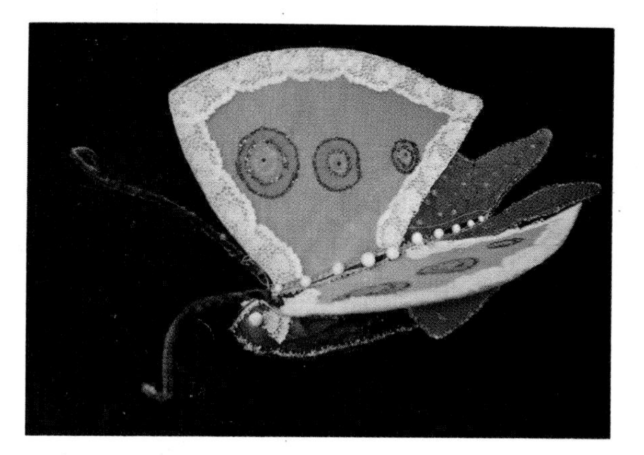

Illus. 344. An insect so beautifully decorated that it must be a royal one. The maroon body, powder-blue wings, purple tail and antennae compose a lovely color scheme. Lace adds delicacy to the wings, and dark blue circles their central design.

PART III: APPENDIX

Message to Teachers

There are two basic approaches to be taken in conducting an art activity—the dictatorial and the creative.

The creative approach, which is the basis for this book, allows students to learn to think for themselves, to make their own decisions, and to be original in the expression of personal ideas. Students are made to feel that *their* ideas are paramount, not how well they imitate someone else's work, nor whom they must please.

Although the teacher demonstrates the basic ideas and construction methods, acquaints the student with the materials and possibilities at hand, and discusses in a general way the project to be undertaken, the student exercises free choice. Choice of subject, method, color, shape, size.

"Do this," and "Do that" can be restricting and inhibiting. A child who may not be able to do one thing, may do another exceedingly well, but he may not be able to do it at all if he is limited in his approach. Freedom rather than frustration is the essence of a truly creative art activity.

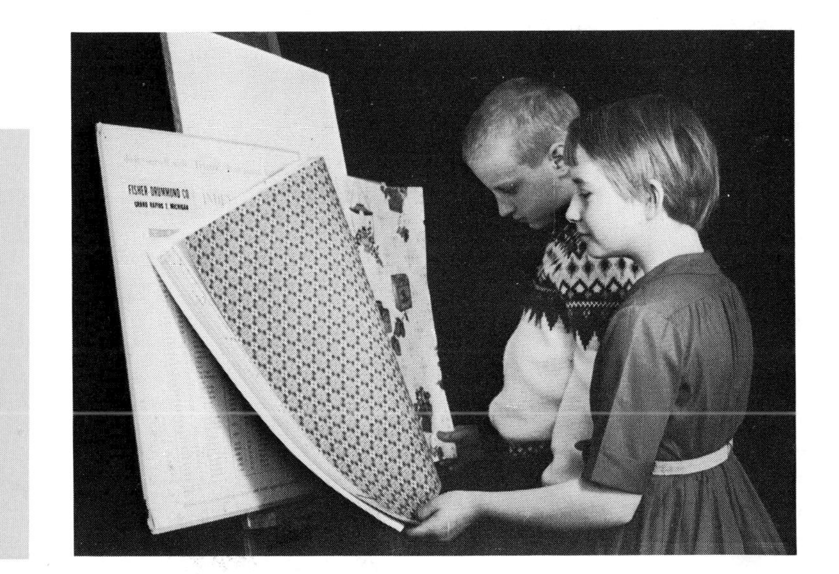

THE AUTHOR

For many years Chester Jay Alkema has taught art to children of the Seymour Christian School, Grand Rapids, Michigan, and the Wyoming Parkview School, Wyoming, Michigan. Since 1959, the author has taught adult art education courses for Michigan State University in East Lansing, Grand Rapids, Benton Harbour and Niles, Michigan. In the spring of 1965, Mr. Alkema joined the art faculty of Grand Valley State College, Allendale, Michigan.

A graduate of Calvin College, Grand Rapids, Michigan, Mr. Alkema received a M.A. in Art and a M.A. in Fine Arts from Michigan State University.

The following is a list of publications by the author:

"Art for the Exceptional Child, A Selected Bibliography by Chester Jay Alkema," *School Arts*, May, 1961.

"Portraits in Depth," *Arts and Activities*, October, 1963.

"The Want Ads Reclassified," *Arts and Activities*, December, 1963.

"Papier Mâché Animals," *School Arts*, March, 1964.

"Weaving in the Elementary Grades," *Arts and Activities*, March, 1964.

"Weaving in the Elementary Grades, Part II," *Arts and Activities*, April, 1964.

"Creative Copper Tooling," *Arts and Activities*, June, 1964.

"Non-Scientific Insect Mobiles," *School Arts*, November, 1964.

"Window Transparencies, Part I: Tissue Hits the Holiday Spot," *Arts and Activities*, November, 1964.

"Window Transparencies, Part II: Flaming Windows Set Christmas Mood," *Arts and Activities*, December, 1964.

"This is a Puppet Any Child Can Make," *Grade Teacher*, February, 1965.

"Magnificent Mosaics," *Arts and Activities*, February, 1965.

"Graph Paper Designs," *Grade Teacher*, April, 1965.

"Kids Create Their Own 'Pop' Art," *Arts and Activities*, May, 1965.

"Papier Mâché," *The Instructor*, September, 1965.

"Masks in Art and History. Part 1: The Development of Masks from Prehistoric to Modern Times," *Arts and Activities*, September, 1965.

"Masks in Art and History. Part 2: Appropriate Methods, Materials and Techniques for Mask-Making," *Arts and Activities*, October, 1965.

"Three-Dimensional Possibilities of Paper," *The Instructor*, May, 1966.

"The Gothic Age Revisited," *Design*, May-June, 1966.

Acknowledgments

The author and publisher wish to extend their appreciation and indebtedness to the many people who contributed in various ways to this book: To Mr. Joseph Brozak, Assistant Superintendent of the Wyoming Public Schools; Mr. Donald O. Martz, Principal, Mrs. Robert McFarland, Mrs. George Aman, Mrs. Raphael Valentine, Mrs. Frank Shivers and Mr. Donald McDougal, teachers, and the children of Wyoming Parkview School for permission to photograph the children and their art products; the art education students of Grand Valley State College and Michigan State University for the many ideas and examples they provided and for their assistance in photographing the art in the book, and especially Mrs. Clarice Claire and others at Grand Valley State College for their invaluable assistance; Miss Marion C. Andros, Supervisor of Art, Kalamazoo (Michigan) Public Schools for the photograph of the paper mosaic on page 44; and to the editors and publishers of *Arts and Activities*, *The Instructor*, *Grade Teacher* and *Design* magazines for the use of the material they originally published.

INDEX